Three Kin...

Simon Stephens began his theatrical career as a tutor in the Young Writers' Programme at the Royal Court Theatre. His plays for theatre include *Bluebird* (Royal Court Theatre, London Upstairs, 1998, directed by Gordon Anderson); *Herons* (Royal Court Theatre Upstairs, 2001); *Port* (Royal Exchange Theatre, Manchester, 2002); *One Minute* (Crucible Theatre, Sheffield, 2003 and Bush Theatre, London, 2004); *Christmas* (Bush Theatre, 2004); *Country Music* (Royal Court Theatre Upstairs, 2004); *On the Shore of the Wide World* (Royal Exchange Theatre and National Theatre, London, 2005); *Motortown* (Royal Court Theatre Downstairs, 2006); *Pornography* (Deutsches Schauspielhaus, Hanover, 2007; Edinburgh Festival/Birmingham Rep, 2008 and Tricycle Theatre, London, 2009); *Harper Regan* (National Theatre, 2008); *Sea Wall* (Bush Theatre, 2008/ Traverse Theatre, Edinburgh, 2009); *Heaven* (Traverse Theatre, 2009); *Punk Rock* (Lyric Hammersmith, London, and Royal Exchange Theatre, 2009); *The Trial of Ubu* (Essen Schauspielhaus/ Toneelgroep Amsterdam, 2010 and Hampstead Theatre, London, 2012); *A Thousand Stars Explode in the Sky* (co-written with David Eldridge and Robert Holman; Lyric Hammersmith, London, 2010); *Marine Parade* (co-written with Mark Eitzel; Brighton International Festival, 2010); *T5* (Traverse Theatre, 2010); and *Wastwater* (Royal Court Theatre Downstairs, 2011). His radio plays include *Five Letters Home to Elizabeth* (BBC Radio 4, 2001) and *Digging* (BBC Radio 4, 2003). His screenwriting includes the two-part serial *Dive* (with Dominic Savage) for Granada/BBC (2009) and a short film adaptation of *Pornography* for Channel 4's 'Coming Up' series (2009). Awards include the Pearson Award for Best New Play, 2001, for *Port*; Olivier Award for Best New Play for *On the Shore of the Wide World*, 2005; and *Theater Heute*'s for *Motortown* (2007), *Pornography* (2008) and *Wastwater* (2011) for Best Foreign Play.

by the same author

Christmas
Country Music
Harper Regan
Herons
Motortown
On the Shore of the Wide World
One Minute
Pornography
Port
Punk Rock
Wastwater *and* T5
The Trial of Ubu

STEPHENS PLAYS: 1
(Bluebird, Christmas, Herons, Port)

STEPHENS PLAYS: 2
(One Minute, Country Music, Motortown,
Pornography, Sea Wall)

STEPHENS PLAYS: 3
(On the Shore of the Wide World,
Marine Parade, Harper Regan, Punk Rock)

with David Eldridge and Robert Holman
A Thousand Stars Explode in the Sky

Simon Stephens

Three Kingdoms

Methuen Drama

Published by Methuen Drama 2012

Methuen Drama, an imprint of Bloomsbury Publishing Plc

1 3 5 7 9 10 8 6 4 2

Methuen Drama
Bloomsbury Publishing Plc
50 Bedford Square
London WC1B 3DP
www.methuendrama.com

First published by Methuen Drama in 2012

Copyright © 2012 Simon Stephens

The author has asserted his rights under the Copyright, Designs
and Patents Act 1988 to be identified as the author of this work

ISBN: 978 1 408 17295 7

A CIP catalogue record for this book is available from
the British Library

Available in the USA from Bloomsbury Academic & Professional,
175 Fifth Avenue/3rd Floor, New York, NY 10010.
www.BloomsburyAcademicUSA.com

Typeset by Country Setting, Kingsdown, Kent
Printed and bound in Great Britain by
MPG Books Ltd, Bodmin, Cornwall

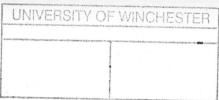

Preface

Interviews conducted in English and edited by Jacqueline Bolton,
April 2012

SIMON STEPHENS (ENGLISH PLAYWRIGHT)

Our readers may be surprised to learn that the published play text they
hold differs considerably from the production of Three Kingdoms
premiered by Sebastian Nübling at NO99 Theatre in Tallinn, Estonia, in
September 2011, with subsequent premieres in Munich, October 2011,
and London, May 2012.

How and why did the premiere depart so significantly from the play text
here authorised for publication?

The play the reader is holding in his or her hand is simply *the*
starting point of this specific production. It is the written text
that Sebastian and his collaborators used to create the
performance text, the show, of the *Three Kingdoms* premiere.
As well as being the writer of that original text, I was also
one of the collaborators in Sebastian's rehearsal room.

Some of the departures were entirely pragmatic. For
complicated reasons. For example, we had to re-cast an actor
to play the lead role of Ignatius half way through rehearsals.
Nick Tennant was originally cast as Charlie, but he was happy
to be re-cast as Ignatius. Ignatius was originally conceived as
bilingual, but Nick couldn't act in German so we had to re-
write. We made Charlie bilingual and cast accordingly.

Also, originally, there weren't enough roles for all the Estonian
actors, as Sebastian very much wanted to work with as many
of the NO99 Company as possible. It was partly because of
this, and partly out of Sebastian's own curiosity, that the
character of The Trickster was created for Risto Kübar. Risto
is a genius of improvisation and he and Sebastian developed a
character inspired by this European mythological figure known
as The Trickster. As in the mediaeval myth, The Trickster
takes many guises and is able to release the subconscious of
those he meets and the underbelly of his world. Sebastian and

I talked a lot about the late films of David Lynch before I wrote the play. We became zealous champions of Lynch's most recent movie, *Inland Empire* [2006]. The Trickster is a Lynchian creation which absolutely emerges from the metabolism of the original play, but he is also a creation of Sebastian's. To publish him as part of the text would seem weird because he was such a product of rehearsal.

But I'd still love to see a version where Ignatius is bilingual, or where some of the lengthier scenes involving Caroline are included. That's why I publish them here.

Many of the changes between the published and performed text resulted from the fusion of our imaginations. I loved Ene-Liise Semper's design, which seemed to understand the atomised, hallucinatory nature of sex and travel and money. The text was edited around her design. I loved the notions and suggestions of dramaturgs Julia Lochte and Eero Epner, who understood our original conceit and, working with the actors, realised it perfectly.

And I knew, to my core, that Sebastian *got* what I wanted to do. This excavation of the thriller genre, this exploration of Europe on its knees, this *atrocity exhibition* of post-colonialism, he just *got* it. We talked a lot before I wrote anything. He sent me films to watch and books to read as I wrote. My text was a response to our shared interest. His production was a response to my text.

What was your role in the collaboration between Sebastian Nübling (director), Ene-Liis Semper (designer), Eero Epner (dramaturg) and Julia Lochte (dramaturg)?

I wasn't the author of this piece; my role was never authorial. I wrote a text that they all responded to. In rehearsal my work was also, weirdly, to respond to my own text. I couldn't afford to be precious about it. I had to dislocate my rehearsing-self from my writing-self. I became merely a privileged reader; I knew this text rather well because I'd written it. But my understanding of it and my word on it was by no means final.

I helped them edit and cut the play. I resisted cutting areas that I thought would be catastrophic if removed. I wrote new sections in the wake of their suggestions or my responses to rehearsal. Eero and Sebastian both enjoy it when text *articulates* idea, rather than text *releasing* idea through sub-text, so I would spend some time writing text that made ideas explicit. Sometimes I would be writing to their command. I loved this. It felt like being a writer on Tin Pan Alley or a Hollywood studio. Sometimes I would give notes to Sebastian about his production. But mainly he ignored me. My main work was about refining the shape of the text and, also, encouraging the British actors not to be frightened when Sebastian behaved in a way that felt counter-intuitive to their culture. They're so used to using the playwright's text as a bible. Sebastian had an instinct to tear it up. I had to let them know that I was happy with that.

In what ways has this international collaboration embodied the hopes for, fears of and concerns over the future of 'Europe' raised by Three Kingdoms? *Is it possible to stage this play without the energy and challenge offered by an multi-cultural cast and creative team?*

I'll only know whether it is possible to do a mono-cultural version when somebody tries to do one. But I think the way we worked yielded immense rewards. Confronting simple differences in attitudes towards speech and language, form and utterance, created greater understanding between acting cultures, I think. It also caused real problems. It led to real bust-ups. But it yielded something extraordinary.

The Anglo-Saxon literalism of the British actors brought nuance and specificity to the language, as well as a humour that is thrilling. The physicality of the Estonians, graced by the legacy of Russian theatre training, takes my breath. The confidence and attack of the German actors stems, I suppose, from their repertory system and creates an incredible energy. The force of Ene-Liis' visual imagination continues to startle me. Sebastian's maverick madness and, actually, his tenderness and irony and suppleness inspire me. Eero and Julia's intellectual rigour sits under everything.

Our refusal to soften or compromise the specifics of each theatre culture created difficulties, but it is also what made the production what it is. In the face of impossible circumstances, and despite ludicrous odds, we kept going and I think we produced something that none of us could have produced in isolation. In that sense, it is exemplary theatre making. It also suggests real possibilities for this frantic, eroding, collapsing, important continent.

SEBASTIAN NÜBLING (GERMAN DIRECTOR)

It was decided from the outset that *Three Kingdoms* would be a three-way collaboration with theatres in Estonia, Germany and England and that the cast would comprise of actors drawn from the ensemble at N099 Theatre, Tallinn, the ensemble at Münchner Kammerspiele, Munich, and England.

What were the challenges of working with actors drawn from different theatre cultures?

First: language. We were rehearsing in English which is for me and for three or four of the cast a language we have learned through pop music, cinema, television series and, years ago, in school. And as we had to discuss and describe to each other attitudes towards, and interpretations of, issues such as art, politics and economics, as well as the quite complex psychic structure of characters and relations, language was a constant source of misunderstanding. Sometimes these misunderstandings were funny or productive and sometimes they were just boring or even responsible for bad feeling. On the other hand, talking so much in a language that is not my native tongue was something very good, kind of satisfying, and it gave me the opportunity to look at myself and the culture I come from through the eyes of the other.

Second: theatre traditions. I was prepared for the differences in theatrical traditions between England, Germany and Estonia: in the British theatre, the play and the playwright come first and many British directors (as far as I can tell, maybe I am wrong and have to apologise to all my British colleagues whose work I do not know!) see themselves as someone who supports the text. In Germany, directors try to invent an autonomous aesthetic with an ambivalent relation to the text. And NO99 are a company that is famous for writing/constructing/sampling plays according to the (political) issues they have to talk about in their country. These approaches are neither better nor worse than one another, just different. But it was a real challenge for all of us to connect to the style of how, for example, our foreign colleagues improvise in the rehearsal room – we had to learn to swim in their water. Fortunately, we managed – even through all the crises – to remain open-minded, or at least able to re-find the state of being open-minded.

Third: the rehearsal room. In Germany we rehearse for eight weeks. I am used to spending a lot of time on improvisation. Through improvisation, a cast creates far more theatrical material than can actually be used in the end. But through these hours of playing together, actors develop a special theatrical language for each production. As a director, I do not have to focus on getting a quick result but can instead take my time and explore many different avenues. My opinion is: a character is defined by what an actor does on stage. This was not very easy for mainly the British actors to understand; they felt lost because we seldom talked about the biography or psychology of a character.

How do the theatre ecologies of Estonia, Germany and England differ from one another and in what ways does this impact upon both the creative process and resulting production?

To answer this question properly would take pages, because they differ on all kinds of levels. Estonia is not a big country, but in proportion to its population it has the highest percentage of theatregoers in Europe after Iceland. The theatre struggles to survive economically but people want to see it, they need theatre as a platform for political discussion. In Germany we have a structure of city theatres with permanent ensembles. An actor/actress is rehearsing four to five productions a season and, as we have a repertory system, it can happen that they are acting in ten different productions which are performed only once or twice a month. So, for us and the Estonians, acting in a production after a three-month interval is a normal thing to do – but not at all for British actors. They are used to focusing on one production throughout both rehearsals and performances, which feels like a luxury to German or Estonian actors who are used to rehearsing a show in the morning from ten until three and then performing another show in the evening six days a week. But they do not have to struggle for the next job like the British freelance system forces everybody to do. And the German theatre system pays better wages, because all of the city theatres are supported by the state. They have to earn only a small percentage of their budget at the box office, but they are permanently under pressure to prove that they are worth the money the state invests in them. Audience attendance is often used as a political argument when it comes to financial negotiations – even in Germany the economic situation is getting harder . . .

In Germany and in Estonia there is no commercial theatre system like the one in London, even though politicians would like to have it: they argue, 'what sells most must be the best' and 'give the people what they want', and theatre practitioners respond: 'no, give the people what they *need*'. And to find out or define or propose what a theatre should present we have the profession of the dramaturg, an unknown species in British theatre. These are people who are, in a way, the theatre's 'department of political philosophy'. They decide which plays will be produced and then team directors with plays and/or playwrights and actors and vice versa.

You have worked with Simon Stephens on several previous productions [Ubu, *a co-production with Toneelgroep Amsterdam, 2010;* Pornography, *a co-production with Schauspiel Hannover, Deutsches Schauspielhaus Hamburg and Theaterformen, 2007; and German-language premieres of Stephens'* Punk Rock, *2010, and* Herons, *2003*]. *What are the rewards of developing a long-term collaborative relationship with a playwright?*

I love most of Simon's plays because in them I find a lot of how I see our world. I feel sort of an excitement when reading a new play of Simon's – I follow him, through his writing, into the darker zones of human existence. In his work, this sense of him leading us to areas of life which we normally try to avoid is combined with a great love of people, and a great sense of humour. And I think that is important to tell or to show in theatre: despair when you look at the state our culture is in, and hope when you see your ability to define your relations to other people.

Directing different plays of Simon's has given me the opportunity to see and to follow the developments in his writing: how he moves from telling a good clean story to texts where he tries to capture more abstract or psychic images. Even his stage directions are a source of inspiration, because he does not try to tell directors and actors what to do but gives poetical or musical hints that we can follow. So, over the years, I have had the chance to come to know the art-cosmos of Simon, and I have had the luck to find a friend in him. And it is on this basis that we have developed projects like *Three Kingdoms*. We planned this on a very rough level together, then Simon wrote it and I tried to find the producers. I would never intervene in the process of writing itself. I admire the act of writing – I could never withstand the loneliness it needs.

EERO EPNER (ESTONIAN DRAMATURG)

Two dramaturgs, yourself and Julia Lochte (German), worked on the premiere of Three Kingdoms *in addition to a designer/art director, Ene-Liis Semper (Estonian) and a music designer, Lars Wittershagen (German). English audiences and readers, however, may not be familiar with the role of dramaturg within rehearsal and production processes. How would you define your relationship with the creative team?*

I think a dramaturg is not a person, but rather a function. And it can be filled by different people. I've seen several times, over and over again, how great actors or video engineers or set designers (Ene-Liis is one of the best dramaturgs I know, for example) can be dramaturgs. How do they do that? They simply lose their normal function and start to do something else. Basically it's a no-man's-land: as a dramaturg, you just shoot everything you see, you have your mouth on your belt and, if necessary (and also – if not), you just pull it out and bang! bang! bang! To be honest, these are mostly blank shots, but the good thing is that your gunfire doesn't leave any signs. It is impossible to say after seeing a show: 'Wow, I really admired the work of the dramaturg, especially this . . . this . . . this . . . eeee . . . you know . . . this . . . well, fuck.'

Theatre is collective art. Don't laugh, I mean it. And everybody in this process has an equal share. It's absolutely old-fashioned and useless to think, feel and underline the hierarchical nature of the theatre. There is no hierarchy. Well, of course there is in today's theatre, but it's a completely fucked-up system. *We did it all together.* A lighting engineer is as equally creative as, let's say, the author (sorry, Simon, don't take it personally, but if there is no light on the stage, then why should I be in the theatre?) So it is impossible to track down different 'contributions'. What is the contribution of an actor? Impossible to describe, actually.

When you first read the play-text of Three Kingdoms, *what were you looking for? How did the creative team approach the play text in rehearsal?*

I guess there is a basic difference between British and German-Estonian theatre thinking. I know British people like the 'Text'. Well, we love it too. But it's never enough. There is a fundamental difference between the Literature and the Theatre: in Literature, the word is word; in Theatre the word becomes flesh. The word is suddenly physical, it has movements, controversial emotions, it smells and flourishes. Of course, when reading the text the reader can also imagine the world around the word (and that's what I did when I read *Three Kingdoms* for the first time in a lonely Munich hotel) but in theatre the word kind of loses its grip: it is still there, but as one element in the manifold stage reality.

A great writer can attempt to control his or her words to the limit, to the point where there is nothing to argue. But in theatre the word is suddenly in the hands of a living person and it becomes vulnerable. I'm ready to fight for every word in, for example, Ian McEwan's oeuvre when *reading* his texts, but I lose any interest in fighting when we *stage* his texts. The word meets now with a human being (an actor) and it might be an embarrassing, painful and lonely process, but it can be also shiny, powerful and tender. We're looking for the latter.

The semiotics of the publicity for Three Kingdoms *at NO99 Theater are interesting: underneath the title of the play the credits are listed as: 'Stephens Nübling Semper', with each name in the same size font. Can you explain what this billing communicates about the division of creative responsibility within Estonian theatre cultures?*

NO99 uses various creative impulses to make theatre and the big aim isn't to illustrate a fiction, as such, but to create a stage reality. Not simply to tell a story, but to create some kind of abstract space where – as Milan Kundera puts it – 'the beauty of the sudden density of life' evolves. Yes, well, this is getting very theoretical now. Basically: for us, the actor is not simply someone who knows his or her lines and who can create some kind of believable figure on the stage: s/he is an artist with his or her autonomy. What s/he does on stage is art. Not *theatre* – but *art*. S/he is not dependent on the text or on the fictional-historical figure s/he embodies: s/he creates a world of his or her own.

So on the poster there should actually be the names of all the actors, sound engineers etc. who made this work. But there is simply no space.

Jacqueline Bolton is a Post-Doctoral Researcher at the University of Reading in conjunction with the Victoria & Albert Museum. She is currently working on a Methuen Student Edition of Simon Stephens' Pornography.

Three Kingdoms

*This play is written with thanks to
the law officers and sex workers who let me talk to them
about their lives in London, Hamburg and Tallinn*

Three Kingdoms was presented in Tallinn at Teater NO99 in Estonia on 17 September 2011, before opening at the Munich Kammerspiele, Germany, on 15 October 2011, and at the Lyric Hammersmith, London, on 3 May 2012. The cast was as follows:

Rasmus Kaljujärv
Risto Kübar
Lasse Myhr
Mirtel Pohla
Jaak Prints
Gert Raudsep
Ferdy Roberts
Steven Scharf
Rupert Simonian
Çigdem Teke
Nicolas Tennant
Tambet Tuisk
Sergo Vares

Director   Sebastian Nübling
Set and Costume Designer   Ene-Liis Semper
Lighting Designer   Stephan Mariani
Composer and Sound Designer   Lars Wittershagen

Characters

DS Ignatius Stone, *English*
DI Charlie Lee, *English*
Tommy White *and* **Receptionist**, *English*
Caroline Stone, **Stephanie Friedmann** *and* **Liisi**, *English /*
  German / Estonian
Steffen Dresner, *German*
Aleksandr Richter, **Georg Kohler** *and* **Klaus Brandt**,
  German
Hele Kachonov, **Kristina Suvi**, **Olya** *and* **Liisu**, *Estonian*
Andres Rebane (**Tom**) *and* **Peeter Koepell**, *Estonian*
Kristen Reims (**Sonny**), *Estonian*
Mart Oper (**Michael**) *and* **Translator**, *Estonian*
Rudie Peiker (**Fredo**), *Estonian*
Mr Petrov *and* **Martin Lemsalu**, *Estonian*

The play is set in England, Germany and Estonia.

In England the characters speak English unless otherwise stated.
In Germany the characters speak German unless otherwise stated.
In Estonia the characters speak Estonian unless otherwise stated.

Simultaneous translation should be displayed on surtitles throughout in
whichever of the three languages is not being spoken by the actors.

Part One: London

*You walk down the street in this city and you've got
Turkish gangsters running your corner shops. Paki
dickless wonders doing your dental work. Coons
running your local councils and white men driving
taxis. You get your moral compass from pop stars.
You get your theology from goalkeepers.*

*Wenn man in dieser Stadt auf die Straße geht, gehört
jeder Kramladen einem türkischen Gangster. Die
Zähne behandelt einem irgendein Paki-Eunuch. Die
Nigger sitzen im Stadtrat, und die Weißen fahren
Taxi. Moralische Orientierung kriegt ihr von
Popstars. Und von Torhütern Theologie.*

*Sa käid mööda linna ringi ja näed, et nurgapealset
poodi peavad türgi gängsterid. Pakistani ilma türata
imeloomad parandavad teil siin hambaid. Mustad
töötavad kohalikes omavalitsuses ja valged mehed
sõidavad taksot. Oma moraalse orientiiri saate
popstaaridelt. Oma teoloogia väravavahtidelt.*

One

Detective Inspector **Charlie Lee**, *Detective Sergeant* **Ignatius Stone** *and* **Tommy White**. *An interview room in the Uxbridge Road branch of Hammersmith and Fulham Police Station.*

Some time.

Charlie What have you done to your hand, Tommy?

Tommy I don't want to talk about it.

Charlie No?

Tommy If you don't mind.

Charlie I don't blame you.

Tommy Thank you.

The men look at **Tommy**. *Some time.*

Ignatius What do you want to talk about, Tommy?

Tommy I don't know what I'm doing here.

Ignatius Is that what you want to talk about?

Tommy I'd like to know what I'm doing here, please.

Charlie We've got all day for that. Why don't you tell us about your hand first, Tommy?

Tommy No, thank you.

Ignatius Did you bandage it yourself?

Charlie 'Cause I don't think you've done a very good job on it, have you, Tommy?

Ignatius Not easy bandaging your own hand. You have to use your teeth very skilfully Tommy, don't you?

Tommy *looks at them. He says nothing.*

Charlie Is that a 'no comment'? Should I take that as a refusal to comment?

Well?

Ignatius   Do you like football, Tommy?

Would you like to chat about football, Tommy? Maybe?

What about music? Do you want to talk about music?

Charlie   Tommy, I promise you we are getting to the business of what in the name of jiminy you're doing here, but first do you want to have a little bit of a chatter about music? Just to warm you up?

I like music, me.

Ignatius   Me too. I love it.

Charlie   Sometimes we have a little song together we like music so much.

Tommy   Is he your boss? Are you his boss? Not much of a boss, is he? More like a clown than a boss.

Ignatius   What music do you like, Tommy?

Tommy, what music do you like?

Tommy, what music do you like?

Tommy   I quite like The Beatles.

Ignatius *and* **Charlie** *share their enjoyment of his response with one another.*

Ignatius   The Beatles?

Charlie   Do you?

Tommy   Yeah.

Charlie   Aren't you a bit young for The Beatles, Tommy?

Tommy   That doesn't matter.

Ignatius   I would say you are. I would say you're far too young to like The Beatles. I would say your mum's too young to like The Beatles, Tommy. Crikey.

Tommy   It doesn't matter.

Ignatius   No?

Charlie   I hate the flipping Beatles.

Tommy   They wrote good songs.

Ignatius   Do you think?

Charlie   I think they wrote poor songs.

Ignatius   What's your favourite Beatles song, Tommy?

Tommy   'I Wanna Hold Your Hand'.

Charlie   Is it?

Ignatius   Ha.

Charlie   That's really poor, that song. I flipping hate it. It gets right on my nerves.

The Beatles!

A pause. **Charlie** *and* **Ignatius** *share a moment. Smile. Then look back to* **Tommy***.*

Charlie   So. Tommy. At 6.55 this morning you, Thomas Jason White, were arrested in your home at Flat 5c of Durban House on the White City Housing Estate in London, W12. Is that right?

Tommy *nods.*

Ignatius   For the tape, the subject nods.

Charlie   The arresting officers were Sergeant Benson and Sergeant Miller from Hammersmith and Fulham. You were taken here to the Shepherd's Bush Police Station on Uxbridge Road. Is that right?

Tommy *nods.*

Ignatius   For the tape, the subject nods.

Charlie   The Custody Sergeant, Sergeant Rashid recorded your arrival at 7.23 this morning.

Tommy   He's fucking lovely.

A beat. The men look at him.

Ignatius   Sorry, Tommy?

Tommy   Sergeant Rashid. Normally desk sergeants are grumpy bastards, he was dead nice.

Charlie   Good.

Ignatius   That's good to hear. That's warming actually, Tommy, that level of respect. It's buoying. I will be sure to pass on your compliments, Tommy. Thank you for that.

Charlie   And it was he who took your fingerprints?

Tommy   Yes.

Charlie   He took your photograph?

Tommy *nods.*

Ignatius   For the tape, the subject nods.

Charlie   And did he take a swab test from inside your mouth?

Tommy *nods.*

Ignatius   For the tape, the subject nods.

Charlie   Were you given the opportunity to make any phone calls?

Tommy   I called my mum.

Charlie   Good thing too.

Ignatius   Don't you live with your mum, Tommy?

Tommy *nods.*

Ignatius   What did you call her for then, Tommy, just to tell her that you got here all right?

Charlie   They like that, mothers do.

Tommy   I just wanted to talk to her.

Charlie   How's your cell?

Tommy   I'm not even going to answer that.

Charlie   They looking after you, are they?

Tommy   Fuck off.

Ignatius   Lovely.

Tommy   I don't know what I'm doing here.

Charlie   You said that.

Ignatius   You kept going on about it.

Tommy   I don't know what I'm meant to have done.

Ignatius   No.

Tommy   I've been here five hours now and nobody's told me what I'm even here for.

Charlie   We realise that.

Tommy   Even Sergeant Rashid wouldn't tell me.

Charlie   He's not allowed to.

Ignatius   I imagine it's a bit unsettling being held here for so long without really knowing what you're being held for, Tommy, isn't it?

Tommy   What am I being charged with?

Charlie   Calm down.

Tommy   I want to see my lawyer. You can't charge me without a lawyer being present in the room.

Ignatius   We can.

Charlie   Tommy, we've not charged you with anything yet.

Ignatius   We could though. If we wanted to. Just for your information.

Charlie   We just want to ask you some questions.

Tommy   Well, what the fuck am I doing down here then? For fucksake! What the fuck did those fuckheads come and fucking wake me up for if you don't want to charge me with anything?

Charlie   Oh! I see what mistake we've made. We should have talked to you at your flat. Shouldn't we? Would you have preferred that?

Tommy   What?

Ignatius   I'm sure your mum wouldn't have minded, would she? Would she, Tommy?

Charlie   Or the neighbours. They're a really nice lot in Durban House from my memory.

Ignatius   They always put on a little welcome dance for us.

Charlie   Have a little party.

Ignatius   They like it best when their neighbours spend a long time talking to the police for no apparent reason and then are left to go about their business as though nothing ever happened. There's nothing they trust more.

Charlie   We should have realised that you would have preferred that.

Ignatius   We're really sorry.

Charlie   Actually it's my responsibility. I made the decision that we should question you here, not DS Stone. So I'm sorry. It was my mistake. He doesn't need to apologise. That's just his nature. He's overly apologetic. Aren't you?

Ignatius   I am sometimes I'm afraid.

Charlie   Do you accept my apology, Tommy? Do you, son? Do you accept my apology?

Tommy *looks away.*

Charlie   Great. Three days ago a sports bag washed up on the west bank of the Chiswick Eyot just south of Chiswick Mall. A lot of debris gets washed up there on account of it being an eyot, an island in the curve of the river, and the tide being fairly, what, strong? At exactly that point. Just north of Castelnau. The most remarkable things.

Ignatius   Dead dogs. Babies' pushchairs. Motorbikes. Shopping trolleys. Etcetera. Etcetera.

Charlie   And because of what was in the bag the police were called. And myself and Detective Sergeant Stone are at the head of the MIT team put in charge of investigating how, that which was found to be contained in the bag came to be there. It was a black waterproof Respro Hump backpack. The kind that is traditionally quite popular with cyclists. It was quite tightly sealed.

But you know that, Tommy, don't you? Don't you, Tommy, eh?

Tommy *doesn't respond.*

Charlie   Now. What you might not know is that there's a former Civil Service Sports Ground in Chiswick. Just east of the railway station. It was bought out this spring by King's House School there. It's quite remarkable the facilities it's got. Rugby pitches. Cricket pitches. Football pitches.

Ignatius   A rowing club.

Charlie   And – and bear with me, Tommy, 'cause this is relevant for you – floodlit tennis courts. And because it used to be owned by the Civil Service for their members and now is being run by the school it has a pretty well updated CCTV facility.

Ignatius   It's considerable.

Charlie   It really is. Even by our standards.

Ignatius   We're impressed.

Charlie   And because of the intact condition that the bag was in, which even for a waterproof bag was surprising, and because of the condition of the contents of the bag and because of the nature of the tides we were able to pretty accurately deduce that the bag had been put into the river no more than two hours before it was washed up. Most probably considerably less than two hours. Whoever put the bag into the river clearly didn't know a great deal about the tide there. And so what we did was we put one or two of our team on to collecting and examining CCTV images of the local river banks for the previous two hours. And to our surprise,

Tommy, guess what they found on the CCTV images coming out of King's House School by the rather beautifully floodlit tennis courts? Here. Have a look.

He passes him an envelope. **Tommy** *takes three photographs from it. He examines them. He tries to not react.*

Ignatius   I always have to fight quite hard, at this stage, to resist the temptation to exclaim 'Gotcha!'

Charlie   Can I ask you, did you not notice the light from the floodlights? Did you not think about that, Tommy? Were you a bit nervous? Is that what it was? I imagine you were, eh?

Ignatius   I wish I could have climbed inside your head, Tommy, at that exact moment just so that I could know exactly why, when you felt the light from the tennis courts shine on your face, you didn't think, 'Hold on a second here, billy-o, I think I'd better find somewhere a bit, what, darker?'

Charlie   So. Tommy. What's the story, morning glory?

Some time.

Tommy   I don't know what you want me to say.

Charlie   Well, why don't we do this. I'll ask you a very simple question and you give me a very simple answer and then, when we're, all of us, happy that we've got the simplest answer possible I'll ask you another question. You'll answer that one and so on and so on until, well, I've run out of questions.

Ignatius   Or it's got jolly late and it's time for us all to go home.

Charlie   OK? OK, Tommy?

Ignatius   Should we take your silence as a sign of approval?

Charlie   So. Pop quiz. Why did you throw the bag in the river?

No response.

Why did you throw the bag in the river?

No response.

Tommy, son, why did you throw the bag in the river?

No response.

Do you accept that that is you, Tommy?

No response.

Tommy, is that you on the photograph?

No response.

Tommy, is that you in the photograph? Sorry, is that a difficult question?

Ignatius   I don't think so.

Charlie   Me neither.

Ignatius   I think it's a clear, simple, closed question that requires a one-word answer of either yes or no.

Charlie   See, that is exactly what I thought. Tommy, is that you in the photograph?

Tommy   Yes.

Charlie   Good. Progress. Yes. Great. Smashing. Super. Great. It's you. So. That's you in the photograph. Off The Promenade scrambling down the east side of the sports field at King's House School in Chiswick with the black Respro backpack in your hand, and that's you throwing the backpack into the river, yes? Is that right, Tommy?

Tommy   Yes.

Charlie   Why were you doing that?

No response.

Why were you throwing the bag in the river, Tommy?

Tommy   Can I see my lawyer please?

Ignatius   Why?

No response.

We're not charging you with anything.

Tommy   I want to see my lawyer, please.

Charlie   We've got photographs. Do you want to see photographs of the – what?

Ignatius   The contents?

Charlie   Good, yes. Do you want to see photographs of the contents of the bag?

Ignatius   Here. Have a look.

Ignatius *passes him another envelope.* **Tommy** *takes a second or two before he makes out what he's looking at, then physically recoils in horror.* **Ignatius** *and* **Charlie** *are mildly entertained.*

Tommy   Fuck. Fuck. Fuck. Fuck. No. No. No. No. No. You're lying. You're fucking. That's sick. That's horrible. That's. Please fuck. No. No. No.

Charlie   Do we need a glass of water?

Tommy   Oh fuck. Oh fuck. Oh fuck. What is wrong with you?

Ignatius   Come on, Tommy, calm down.

Charlie   Do you need a glass of water, Tommy?

Tommy   You're sick, man. You're making this up.

Ignatius   What, Tommy? That was what was taken out of the bag. What are you trying to say, Tommy, that it was a different bag?

Tommy   I don't know.

Charlie   Are you suggesting that we made this up?

Tommy   No. I don't know.

Charlie   Then what on earth are you trying to say, Tommy?

Tommy   I didn't know. I didn't know. I didn't know, OK? I didn't know.

Charlie *and* **Ignatius** *take a moment to cast each other almost theatrical glances.*

Ignatius   You didn't know what, Tommy?

Tommy   I didn't know what was in the bag.

Ignatius   What do you mean, you didn't know what was in the bag?

Tommy   I mean I didn't know what was inside the bag. I met. There was a man.

Charlie   There was a what?

Tommy   There was a man.

Ignatius   A man?

Charlie   Listen, Tommy. This is getting a bit shall we say random?

Ignatius   Well, dislocated.

Charlie   A little dislocated.

He walks out of the room.

Ignatius (*into the tape*)   Detective Inspector Lee leaves the room.

Tommy   Where's he going? Where the fuck is he going now?

Ignatius *stares at him for a bit. Smiles slightly.*

Ignatius   Look at you.

Tommy   What about me?

Ignatius   When was the last time you had a bath, Tommy?

Tommy   Fuck off.

Ignatius   Had a nice pie or something like that, Tommy, yes?

Tommy   Where's he gone to?

Ignatius   I don't know.

Tommy   Can he just do that? Can he just walk out like that?

Ignatius   If he wants to.

Tommy   Can I see a doctor, please?

Ignatius   What do you want to see a doctor for?

Tommy   I think I need to, don't you?

Ignatius   Did you see one when you came in?

Tommy   Yes I did, yes.

Ignatius   And you'll see him again when we finish and he's a perfectly neutral doctor, he's not on anybody's side – he'll check you over and if he finds any evidence of anything that causes him concern –

Tommy   There won't be, will there?

Ignatius   What?

Tommy   Any evidence.

Ignatius   Are you cold?

Tommy   Yes.

Ignatius   Would you like a blanket?

Tommy   Fuck off.

Ignatius   Do you find this all a little bit tiring sometimes, Tommy? Do you just sometimes wish this could just blinking well stop?

Tommy   Fuck off.

Ignatius   See, what worries me about you now, Tommy, is that it won't. It never will.

Tommy   Fuck off.

Ignatius   Don't swear.

Tommy   Fuck you.

Ignatius   It's ignorant, Tommy. It doesn't become you.

Charlie *returns to the room. He is holding a Mars bar and a glass of water.*

Ignatius (*into the tape*)   Detective Inspector Lee re-enters the interview room.

Charlie *gives* **Tommy** *the water and the Mars bar.*

Charlie   Here.

Tommy   Thank you.

He eats the Mars bar.

Charlie   Better?

Tommy *glares at him.*

Charlie   Finish your water.

Charlie *and* **Ignatius** *watch* **Tommy** *drink his water. He puts the cup down. He looks at them for a time.*

Tommy   I was in the William Morris.

Charlie   On King Street?

Tommy   That's right.

Charlie   When was this?

Tommy   Last Tuesday.

Charlie   The twenty-first of May?

Tommy   I don't know. The Tuesday we just had. The last one we had.

Ignatius   The twenty-first of May, yes.

Tommy   I was having a, a, a, a beer.

Charlie   A beer?

Tommy   Yes.

Ignatius   That's not altogether that remarkable is it, Tommy? Not in a pub. That's quite common, I think.

Charlie   Were you on your own?

Tommy   I was, yes.

Charlie   Right.

There is some time. **Charlie** *and* **Ignatius** *regard* **Tommy** *slightly expectantly.*

Ignatius   And then what happened?

Tommy   I was drinking my beer and I looked up and there was a man sat next to me.

Ignatius   A man.

Tommy   That's right.

Ignatius   Again not really all that unusual for a pub when you think about it.

Charlie   Men. Beer. Pubs. They kind of go hand in hand a bit, don't they?

Tommy   You don't need to be fucking clever, all right? I'm telling you the truth.

Charlie *and* **Ignatius** *allow* **Tommy** *to continue.*

Tommy   He sits there for about five minutes and he doesn't have a drink or anything and it's odd because there are other spare tables.

Charlie   OK.

Tommy   And after about five minutes I do, I, I look at him and he says to me, 'Hello, Tommy.'

Charlie   Had you met him before?

Tommy   No.

Charlie   Had you met him before, Tommy?

Tommy   I told you I hadn't, no.

Ignatius   Had you seen him before maybe?

Tommy   No. I don't think I had.

Charlie   But he knew your name?

Tommy   That's right.

Charlie   He said it to you?

Tommy   He said 'Hello Tommy.'

Ignatius   And what did you say?

Tommy   I didn't say anything.

Charlie   And then what happened?

Tommy   He asked me if I wanted to make a hundred pounds in money.

Charlie   A hundred pounds?

Tommy   Yes.

Charlie   Is that what he paid you?

Tommy   So I said, 'Who the fuck are you?' and he starts chuckling. It's like he's a bit mentally ill 'cause he just does all this giggling and chuckling and stuff. He's not English.

Charlie   What?

Tommy   He's not an English person.

Charlie   How could you tell?

Tommy   'Cause he spoke funny.

Ignatius   Maybe he was disguising his voice –

Tommy   He spoke a different language.

Charlie   When?

Tommy   He said something to himself in a language that wasn't English.

Charlie   You don't happen to know what language, do you, Tommy?

Tommy   It sounded German.

Ignatius   German?

Tommy   It was like German or Russian or something. Not French.

Charlie   Do you speak much French, do you, Tommy?

Tommy *looks at him. Says nothing.*

Charlie   He didn't tell you his name?

Tommy   No.

Charlie   And you didn't ask him?

Tommy   No.

Ignatius   What else did he say to you apart from saying 'Hello Tommy' and asking you if you wanted to earn a hundred pounds and talking to himself in a language that definitely wasn't French?

Tommy   He said to me, 'If you go and throw this bag in the river I'll pay you a hundred pounds.' He told me not to open it. He told me not to ask what was inside it. I said, 'Give me the money now, then.' And he did.

Ignatius   Did he?

Tommy   Yeah.

Ignatius   He just gave you a hundred pounds.

Tommy   Yeah.

Ignatius   Just like that?

Tommy   Yeah, just like that.

Charlie   And then what happened?

Tommy   Then all he did was stand up and walk away.

Ignatius   Leaving you with the bag in the William Morris?

Charlie *and* **Ignatius** *consider* **Tommy** *for a time. He had been roundly fucked.*

Tommy   And I think, fuck. Well, I'd better get shot of it now then, hadn't I? I picked it up. I was going to look inside it in case it was like a lot of money or something. Or like drugs or guns or something.

Ignatius   Rugs?

Tommy   Drugs. With a 'd'.

Ignatius   Right.

Tommy   But I kind of thought if you had money or drugs or guns or anything else nice you wouldn't want to throw it in the river, would you? And so I thought it was probably pretty horrible. Whatever was inside it. So I decided not to look at it. I thought I should just leave it in the pub, but I like that pub. I go there all the time. And if it was something bad that could get them in trouble and anyway they know me and they knew where I was sitting. And so I decided to do what he said and I walked out of the pub with the bag and I walked away and I found the river and I walked along it and I was a bit worried so I just walked and walked and walked until I got to the, The Promenade in Chiswick and then I just, I did throw it in.

Ignatius   He must have been looking for you.

Tommy   I don't know.

Charlie   He must have asked somebody, 'Do you know anybody so stupid that they'll throw a bag in the River Thames for me and not open it up to see what's inside and not ask me any questions as long as I pay him a hundred pounds?' He must have asked somebody that and they must have told him about you. That's right, isn't it, Tommy? Have you ever seen a corpse before, Tommy?

Tommy   No.

Charlie   It has an amazing smell. You never really forget it, Tommy, you know?

Ignatius   It's like an old butcher's shop but a thousand times worse.

Charlie   And even though the bag was closed tightly this head had been in the river for two hours by the time it was found.

Ignatius   She stank.

Charlie   We've got thirty people working on this case, Tommy, and they're some of them sitting outside this very room perched on their little desk waiting to hear what we find out from you.

Ignatius   And some of them share desks.

Charlie   That's right.

Ignatius   They hot-desk.

So there's not a great deal of room.

Charlie   And there are some of them, Tommy, there are, there are some of them who are completely convinced that it was you who did this to her.

Tommy   What?

Charlie   I'm only telling you what they think. I'm trying my hardest to be honest with you. And they're a bit, what?

Ignatius   Unreconstructed.

Charlie   Yes. Precisely. They're a bit unreconstructed, some of these chaps, and really, Tommy, it was the best I could do to stop them from coming in here and bouncing your head up and down off the floor because that's what they really, really wanted to do. So. I'm telling you the truth. Why don't you tell me the truth, Tommy?

Tommy   I am telling you the truth.

Charlie   Was this how you hurt your hand, Tommy. Doing this to her?

Tommy   What?

Charlie   When did you meet her?

Tommy   Who? What? Who are you talking about?

Charlie   When did you meet her, Tommy?

Tommy   I never met her.

Charlie   How long have you known her, Tommy?

Tommy   I don't know her. Who? I never met her.

Charlie   Whereabouts did you meet her though, Tommy?

Tommy   Did you not hear what I said?

Ignatius   Was she your girlfriend?

Tommy   Did you not hear what I said?

Ignatius   Was she your girlfriend?

Tommy   Are you not listening to me?

There is some time.

Charlie   Do you know what the maximum sentence for perverting the course of justice is, Tommy?

Ignatius   It's life imprisonment, isn't it?

Tommy   It's what?

Ignatius   It is, Tommy. It's life, lad.

Tommy *recoils. He shivers slightly.*

Charlie   Are you all right? Are you all right, Tommy? Do you need a break or something?

They watch him struggle to pull himself together. He talks very quietly.

Tommy   I'm a bit worried.

Charlie   Are you?

Tommy   I'm a bit worried about what's going to happen to me.

Charlie   Yeah.

Ignatius   It's a horrible feeling. Worry. Isn't it?

Charlie   I think so.

Ignatius   It gets right inside you.

Tommy   I really.

Ignatius   What?

Tommy   I'm trying to.

Ignatius   What?

Tommy   Like, be good.

Ignatius   Are you?

Tommy   And I really am telling you the truth and the whole truth and nothing but the truth.

Charlie   Yeah.

Tommy   But every time I try to be good. Something happens and I just –

Charlie   What?

Ignatius   Do you lose it?

Tommy *looks at* **Ignatius** *for a time like he's completely understood him.*

Two

DI **Charlie Lee** *and DS* **Ignatius Stone**. **Charlie***'s office.*

Charlie   How's the energy levels?

Ignatius   I could kill a sausage roll. And another coffee.

Charlie   I've started sweating. I always do after about sixteen hours. It's really unpleasant.

Ignatius   Can I recommend Vichy Homme?

Charlie   What?

Ignatius   It's a French deodorant. It's terrific.

Charlie   Thank you, Ignatius, that's, well, thoughtful of you.

Ignatius   It's completely my pleasure.

You know what I've been mulling on, Charlie?

Charlie   Surprise me.

Ignatius   Exactly what it is that's so horrible about cutting somebody's head off.

Charlie *examines* **Ignatius**.

Charlie   Well, I bet it really hurts.

Ignatius   But if you cut somebody's leg off it would hurt them, to be fair.

Charlie   It would in all probability kill them as well.

Ignatius   If you chopped their arm off the likelihood is that it might.

Charlie   –

Ignatius   Clearly somebody wanted to do more to this girl –

Charlie   Vera Petrova.

Ignatius   Aka Vera Chislova, aka Vera Kukk, than just hurt her. Or kill her.

Charlie   Do you know, this is exactly the kind of conversation I was hoping to have at this time of the morning.

Ignatius   When you remove somebody's head you remove two things from their body, yes? You remove their face and you remove their brain, yes?

Charlie   And their hair.

Ignatius   Now if you remove somebody's face you remove their identity, yes?

Charlie   And their nose. Let's go home.

Ignatius   If you remove somebody's brain you remove their consciousness. Well, actually what you do is you separate their consciousness from their corporality, from their body. So we have somebody whose intention is to punish this girl in the most extreme way imaginable. In the fifteenth century they used to display heads of traitors on spikes on Bridge Gate. Why did they do that?

Ignatius   Comic effect?

Charlie   These people. They're really, really quite cross.

Charlie   Clearly.

Ignatius   And can I say?

Charlie   What?

Ignatius   It's not easy.

Charlie   No.

Ignatius   Taking somebody's head off. Not easy at all. Did you actually watch the execution of Nick Berg? Goodness gracious me, it took a bit of effort.

Charlie   Are you not tired?

Ignatius   I've never seen one before. A head.

Charlie   They were all the rage in the late eighties.

Ignatius   They're a lot smaller than you imagine, aren't they?

Charlie   They always look surprisingly like a cauliflower to me.

Three

Ignatius Stone *and* **Caroline Stone**. *Their flat.*

Ignatius   You're awake.

Caroline   Not wildly.

Ignatius   What are you doing awake?

Caroline   I don't really know. I'm not altogether sure. I'm completely exhausted.

Ignatius   You weren't waiting up for me, were you?

Caroline   Don't be stupid.

Ignatius   You don't look it.

Caroline   What?

Ignatius   Completely exhausted.

Caroline   I really do, you know?

Ignatius   Go to bed then.

Caroline   In a bit.

Ignatius   Would you like a cup of tea?

Caroline   Not at one o'clock in the morning, Ig. That would be maniacal.

Ignatius   Hot chocolate.

Caroline   No thank you.

Ignatius   Maniacal's a bit strong. Herbal infusion.

Sorry.

Caroline   No. I'm sorry. I'm a bit distracted. How was work?

He smiles at her. Decides not to answer.

Ignatius   How was your day?

Caroline   Fucking magical.

Ignatius   What did you do?

Caroline   Found this.

She holds up the damaged remains of a blue flower. He smells it.

Ignatius   What is it?

Caroline   That's what I'm trying to figure out.

Ignatius   It looks like a peony.

Caroline   You can't get a blue peony.

Ignatius   Course you can.

Caroline   Not this blue you can't.

Ignatius   Where did you find it?

Caroline   In the back garden. Where do you think?
What?

Ignatius   Sorry. Hey. Caroline.

Caroline   What?

Ignatius   Nothing. I'm not sleepy in the least.

Caroline   You should have a shower. That'll help.

Ignatius   I know.

Caroline   You smell a bit.

Ignatius   I don't, do I?

Caroline   You do actually. Have you been eating sausage rolls again?

Ignatius   One. I had one.

Caroline   See.

Ignatius   What?

Caroline   I knew it.

Ignatius   Knew what?

Caroline   Sausage rolls. You can't get a sausage roll past me, Sonny-Jim.

He looks at her for a short time.

Ignatius   We should go out, you know, me and you? Go and get something decent to eat.

Caroline   Now?

Ignatius   I'd like to go somewhere and spend an absurd amount of money on getting something really fucking ridiculous to eat with you.

Caroline   You wouldn't.

Ignatius   Powdered Anjou pigeon. Macarated strawberries. Roast fois grois. Snail porridge.

Caroline   Have you gone totally mad?

Ignatius   Come to bed.

Caroline   I will. I promise.

Ignatius   I don't mean for a fuck.

Caroline   God no.

Ignatius   I'd just like you to go to sleep at the same time as me.

Caroline   I will.

Ignatius   Just for once I'd like that.

Caroline   What are you talking about?

Ignatius   I'm sorry. I'm going to go and have a shower.

Caroline   Right.

Ignatius   Do you know what else we should do?

Caroline   What?

Ignatius   Go for an enormous walk. This weekend.

Caroline   OK.

Ignatius   Walk down to the river.

Caroline   From here?

Ignatius   That's exactly what we should do. We should walk down to the river. I'd go with you.

Caroline   Ig.

Ignatius   We could steal a speedboat and just jolly well leave.

Caroline   G'night, Iggy.

Ignatius   Don't you find me funny any more?

Caroline   I want to find out what flower this is. I need to do an Ocado. I've got to answer my emails. I'm really tired.

Ignatius   It might be a blue tuberose. They're from Mexico originally. Claude Manet painted them, I think.

I love you, by the way.

Four

The next morning. **Charlie***'s office.*

Charlie   Peeter.

Peeter   Charlie.

Charlie   How the devil are you?

Peeter   Very well. Very busy.

Charlie   Very good.

Peeter   Yes.

Charlie   Peeter, this is my colleague, Detective Sergeant Ignatius Stone. Ignatius, this is Peeter Koepell from the Home Office.

Ignatius   How very nice to meet you.

Peeter   And yes, me too. Yes. Is that really your name?

Ignatius   Well, it's not a stage name.

Peeter   No?

Ignatius   It's not a pseudonym.

Peeter   Ha. It's nice. It's a nice name. It's very old. It's Latin. It means 'ardent, passionate, burning'.

So. I've done a preliminary. I'll deliver a full report by the end of the week. But here we are for now. Although there is very little we can tell from such a limited body part especially after a period of time in the water, however brief that period may have been, so don't expect too much development in the full and final report. There are certain things I want to draw your attention to.

As expected the deceased is female.

Ignatius   Very good.

Peeter   She is twenty-eight years old.

Ignatius   Caroline's age.

Peeter *and* **Charlie** *look at* **Ignatius**, *confused.*

Charlie   His wife.

Peeter   From the size of her cranium we would estimate her height as being somewhere between five foot three and five foot five. Impossible to tell her weight really, but there is little evidence of surplus fatty tissues around the jowls so I would imagine ordinary or low body-weight, somewhere around the region of a hundred and twenty pounds. Some points of minor interest. Firstly she was HIV positive. So she would have died anyway, yes? This just speeded up the process, ha? Not funny?

Ignatius   Not that funny.

Charlie   A bit funny, but not really all that funny, no.

Peeter   OK. Secondly there are traces of rohypnol in her bloodstream along with traces of alcohol and traces of heroin. Heroin, as you know, will stay in the blood stream for not much more than twenty-four hours. Thirdly and most remarkably, we found traces of semen in her hair. Which after two hours in the water is pretty fucking astonishing, yes? Two further things that it's worth considering. One odd thing. The quality of the dental work is very high. Higher than you'd get on the NHS. Definitely higher than you'd get in Russia. Unless you were in the position to pay for it.

Charlie   Which she might have been.

Peeter   Maybe. But consider this: She's had dental surgery in the past five years. Pre-prosthetic surgery to provide better anatomy to implant dentures in. Which is unusual in somebody so young. And what we can tell is that the surgery has been carried out by a different surgeon than the dentist who popped her fillings in. There aren't many countries where dentoalveolar surgery is taught as a specialism. But there is one quite interesting one. Estonia.

Ignatius   She comes up on HOLMES as being Russian.

Peeter   She might be.

Ignatius   She might have just had an Estonian dentist.

Charlie   Or visited Estonia to have her teeth done.

Ignatius   Computer Operations found fourteen pornographic films in which she stars, produced by a Russian company called StudentSexParties.com.

Peeter   What language does she speak?

Ignatius   What?

Peeter   In the films, what language does she speak?

Ignatius   I don't know.

Peeter   You've not watched them?

Ignatius   No.

Peeter   Yeah, you probably should.

Now. The juice. From the state of decomposition, even having spent a period of time in the water we can estimate the time of death fairly confidently to have been within thirty-six hours of the bag being discovered. The cause of the death, we are pretty certain, was massive blood loss caused by her decapitation. There are wounds at the top of her head on both the right- and the left-hand side that suggest that the head had been held in some kind of vice.

Charlie   The wounds are caused by vice marks?

Peeter   Probably from a fairly standard forge-steel vice. There are traces of iron deposit in the skin under the wounds.

The question being, ladies: why would they hold her head in a vice?

Ignatius   To keep it still.

Charlie   So she was alive at the time of decapitation.

Peeter   We've not had a full tissue examination as yet, so hard to say for certain, but distinctly possible. Yes.

Charlie   But it would be much easier, wouldn't it? To decapitate a corpse than to decapitate a living person?

Ignatius   I would have thought so.

Charlie   More expedient. Less hassle.

Ignatius   Comparitively less messy.

Charlie   Unless you were making a point.

Ignatius   But if you were making a point, why would you put her head in the river?

Charlie   If you kept the body.

Ignatius   Or if you had an audience?

Peeter   I honestly have no fucking idea.

Ignatius   No.

Charlie   Nor should you.

Peeter   It's not really my specialism.

Charlie   Of course it isn't.

Peeter   Surely that's your job.

Ignatius   Absolutely, it is.

Peeter   And they used a saw. To decapitate her.

Charlie   A sword?

Peeter   No. A saw. Not a sword. A saw. And not a chain saw. Like a large hand saw. I think quite a blunt one. You can tell from the way the spinal column's cut. It's jagged. They had to make several attempts. They sawed it, not sliced it.

Five

DI **Charlie Lee**, *DS* **Ignatius Stone**, **Hele Kachonov**
and a **Translator** *in a back room of a terraced house in Barons
Court, West London. The* **Translator** *speaks in Russian and* **Hele**
in an Estonian-dialect Russian, unless otherwise stated.

Ignatius   We brought you some cake.

Translator   We bought you some cake.

Hele *doesn't respond or move. The three men continue to look at her.*

Ignatius   It's really nice.

Translator   It's really nice.

Ignatius   We both had a slice on our way here, didn't we?

Charlie   We did. Yes.

Ignatius   And I'm right, aren't I?

Charlie   He is.

Ignatius   It is lovely, isn't it?

Charlie   Delicious.

Translator   They both had a slice and agree it's lovely.

Ignatius   Here. Take the cake. You can have that even if
you don't tell us anything. You can have it as a little gift.

Translator   You can have the cake even if you don't say
anything.

Ignatius   We won't even claim it back on expenses, Hele.
We're just giving it to you as a gesture of friendship.

You can eat it now or you can save it and eat it later.

Translator   You can take it and not eat it until later.

Ignatius   OK? Is that OK, Hele?

Translator   Is that OK?

She takes the cake. She looks at it. She eats it. They watch her.

Charlie   You're not in any trouble.

Translator   You're not in any trouble.

Ignatius   We're here to talk to you about Vera.

Translator   We're here to talk to you about Vera.

Charlie   Do you remember her, Hele?

Translator   Do you remember her, Hele?

A brief time.

Hele   No.

Charlie   She worked at Becklow Road with you. Last year.

Translator   She worked at Becklow Road with you. Last year.

Charlie   Do you remember working at Becklow Road, Hele?

Translator   Do you remember working at Becklow Road, Hele?

Charlie   Hele, do you remember working at Becklow Road?

Translator   The same question is repeated.

Charlie   Hele, do you remember working at Becklow Road?

Translator   The same question is repeated.

Hele   No.

Ignatius   Are you really sure?

Translator   Are you really sure?

Hele   I'm certain.

Translator (*in English*)   I'm certain.

Charlie   You were registered at the same address, Hele. And arrested for soliciting on the same date.

Translator   You were registered at the same address, Hele. And arrested for soliciting on the same date.

Ignatius   I mean, come on, Hele, I know we all lead busy lives but surely that's the kind of thing people remember, isn't it?

Charlie   I'd remember it if it happened to me.

Translator   It seems likely that most people would remember something like that happening to them. Certainly we would.

Charlie   OK. I can imagine you're nervous.

Translator   I imagine you're nervous.

Charlie   Are you nervous, Hele?

Ignatius   Are you a bit frightened even?

Translator   Are you nervous or frightened?

Hele   No.

Charlie   Who do you work for, Hele?

Translator   Who do you work for, Hele?

Hele   What are you talking about?

There is a brief pause. The Estonian dialect causes the **Translator** *to hesitate.*

Translator (*in English*)   What are you talking about?

Charlie   Who do you pay your rent to?

Translator   Who do you pay your rent to?

Charlie   Where is he, Hele?

Translator   Where is he, Hele?

Ignatius   Because if he finds out we've been round I imagine he might be a bit cross with you, wouldn't he, Hele?

Translator   Because if he finds out we've been round I imagine he might be a bit cross with you, wouldn't he, Hele?

Charlie   Look. Why don't we do this? You're not under arrest. You're not charged with anything. We can go away and get a warrant and arrest you if you want us to, or you could just answer our questions without going through any of that complete nonsense.

Translator   You're not under arrest. You're not charged with anything. We can go away and get a warrant and arrest you if you want us to or you could just answer our questions without going through any of that.

Charlie   You could even nod or shake your head and we'd accept that not as evidence, but just as something to believe and to follow up on.

Translator   You could even nod or shake your head and we'd accept that not as evidence, but just as something to believe and to follow up on.

Ignatius   Because what happened to Vera was really bad, Hele, wasn't it? And there is a considerable part of my sensibility that finds myself really quite committed to finding whoever did that to her and making sure they spend really quite a long time in jail.

Translator   What happened to Vera was really bad and whoever carried that out should be jailed for years.

Ignatius   Did you understand me?

Translator   Did you understand me?

Hele *nods.*

Ignatius   When was the last time you saw her?

Translator   When was the last time you saw her?

Ignatius   When was the last time you saw her, Hele?

Translator   The same question is repeated.

Ignatius   Hele, when was the last time you saw her?

Translator   The same question is repeated.

Ignatius   Was it within the past six months?

Translator   Was it within the six months?

Charlie   You can nod or shake your head.

Translator   You can nod or shake your head.

She nods.

Ignatius   Was it in the past month?

Translator   Was it within the past month?

She nods.

Ignatius   Was it in the past two weeks?

Translator   Was it within the past two weeks?

She nods.

Ignatius   Was she living here?

Translator   Was she living here?

She shakes her head.

Charlie   Do you know where she was living?

Translator   Do you know where she was living?

She doesn't move.

Charlie   Can you tell us? Can you tell us, Hele, where Vera was living?

Translator   The same question is repeated.

She doesn't move.

Ignatius   Was she working for the same person you work for?

Translator   Was she working for the same person you work for?

She doesn't move.

Ignatius   Was she working for the same person you work for?

Translator   The same question is repeated.

Hele *gives the tiniest nod of the head.*

Ignatius   Who is he?

Translator   Who is he?

She doesn't respond.

Ignatius   Who is he, Hele?

Translator   Who is he, Hele?

She doesn't respond.

Ignatius   Hele, who was Vera working for?

Hele (*in English*)   My boyfriend.

Charlie   Very good. That's very good. Thank you, Hele.

Translator   Very good. Thank you.

Ignatius   What's his name? Hele, what's he called? Your boyfriend?

Translator   What is your boyfriend's name?

She doesn't respond.

Ignatius   Are you worried that somebody's going to see you? Or that somebody's going to find out that you were talking to us?

Translator   Are you worried that somebody's going to see you? Or that somebody's going to find out that you were talking to us?

She doesn't respond.

Ignatius   Because nobody will. I promise you.

Translator   Nobody will. I promise.

Ignatius   And if they do we will kill them. Metaphorically speaking.

Translator   And if we do we'll kill them.

Charlie   Yes. That was just a metaphor.

Translator   That was just a metaphor about killing them.

Charlie   We're the biggest gang in London.

Translator   We're the biggest gang in London.

Ignatius   We're the biggest gang in Europe.

Translator   We're the biggest gang in Europe.

Charlie   We've got twelve helicopters.

Translator   We've got twelve helicopters.

Ignatius   We've got five speedboats.

Translator   We've got five speedboats.

Charlie   We get free access to the transport system.

Ignatius   Does – what's he called? Your boyfriend, what's he called?

Translator   What is your boyfriend called?

Some time and then:

Hele (*in English*)   He's called Aleksandr.

Charlie   Aleksandr?

Ignatius   Is he really called Aleksandr?

Translator   Is he really called Aleksandr?

Charlie   You're not lying to us are you, Hele?

Translator   You're not lying to us are you, Hele?

Hele   No, I'm not fucking lying.

Translator   No, I'm not fucking lying.

Charlie   Right. Aleksandr.

Ignatius   Hele, does Aleksandr have free access to the London Underground?

Translator   Does Aleksandr have free access to the London Underground?

Hele   No, of course he doesn't.

Translator   No, of course he doesn't.

Ignatius   No, course he doesn't. You honestly have nothing to worry about.

Translator (*in English*)   She's not Russian.

Ignatius   I'm sorry?

Translator (*in English*)   She's not Russian. Her dialect isn't Russian. She's Lithuanian. Or Bulgarian. Latvian. She's not Russian.

Six

DI **Charlie Lee**, *DS* **Ignatius Stone** *and* **Aleksandr Richter**. *In the reception area outside* **Richter**'s *office.*

Aleksandr   What's she done?

Ignatius   Who?

Aleksandr   This stupid cunt.

Charlie   She's not done a great deal, Aleksandr.

Ignatius   Well, not lately at least. She's been defined by her inertia.

Aleksandr   Are you trying to frighten me?

Charlie   No.

Aleksandr   Because this isn't the kind of thing that scares me, you fucking piece of fuck.

Charlie   Our intention wasn't to frighten you, it was to try to solicit honesty.

Ignatius   To get you to tell the truth, Aleksandr, really was all we were hoping to do.

Charlie   Sometimes fear is actually counter-productive.

Ignatius   People can clam up.

Charlie   So.

When did you last see her?

Ignatius   When did you last see her, Aleksandr?

When the fuck did you last see her?

Charlie   Did you just swear?

Ignatius   I know. I'm really sorry.

Charlie   He never swears. He's just a little bit wound up.

It's your fault, to be honest, Aleksandr.

Stop smirking. It's not impressive. You've a remarkably ugly face and the smirk is the expression which least suits it I have to say.

Ignatius   Can I just stop you there and exclaim how right you are.

In what way?

Charlie   I've been so distracted by the matter at hand that I've not really been paying much attention to just how ugly his face is, but crikey, it's horrible isn't it.

Aleksandr   I'm getting really bored of this.

Charlie   Bored?

Aleksandr   The pair of you is unbelievably boring.

Ignatius   Gosh.

Charlie   That's a bit rude Aleksandr.

Aleksandr   She was shit.

Charlie   I'm sorry?

Aleksandr   She made shit money. She had a shit cunt. She fucked like a dead cow. She stank. She was lazy. She never stopped complaining. She was rude to the customers. She never cleaned out her cunt. The clients could smell other men inside her.

She deserved to die. She deserved to get her head cut off. She was a stinking rotten piece of fucking meat. She was good for one thing. And even that she fucked up.

But what I want to know is what fucking right has somebody who wears shoes like you got to ask me about my work? I'm sorry, jiminy-cricket, it doesn't work like that. You know how it works? I buy the suit. I fuck what I want. You dumb fuck-holes nod quietly and say 'Yes massir' as softly as you can and take your fucking shoes off at my front door. Soft-hearted monkey twats let clowns like you two and cunts like Petrova vote and what fucking happens?

You walk down the street in this city and you've got Turkish gangsters running your corner shops. Paki dickless wonders doing your dental work. Coons running your local councils and white men driving taxis. You get your moral compass from pop stars. You get your theology from goalkeepers. The human race is like weed. It grows. And then it flowers. It takes over a space and then it kills it. It rots and it dies. Unless you have people like me and my grandfather and my great-grandfather and my great-great-grandfather telling all the stupid dick-fuckers what to do and where to go and what to think and what the fuck to wear.

Dignity is not inherent. Human beings are not equal. No right is inalienable. We are not a fucking family.

Everything I value in this country has been made a mockery of by people like you.

In my darker moments I find I would like to punish you in the cruellest way imaginable. In those moments I feel I would like to grind broken glass up your arsehole. In those moments it's like I would like to stab your eyes with metal sticks. I would like to tear your skins off and burn you, repeatedly. I would like to stamp on your skulls until they shatter and then stamp more to the point that I grind your pissy brains to salt.

It takes **Ignatius** *and* **Charlie** *a moment to digest these ideas.*

Charlie   So we're going to charge you.

Aleksandr   For what?

Charlie   Well, I say we, actually what we're doing is acting on behalf of Her Majesty's Government.

Aleksandr   This is fucking ridiculous. You're a pair of fucking comedians.

Charlie   We're really not.

Aleksandr   You fucking are, you fucking cock-faced cunts.

Ignatius   It's taken me a while to properly visualise that image in my mind.

Charlie   Me too.

Ignatius   It seems, what? In some way, contradictory?

Aleksandr   I want to speak to my lawyer.

Charlie   Really? Do you, Aleksandr? Because when you've been charged for committing murder it really is something –

Aleksandr   Are you going to try to stop me from calling a lawyer? Because that would be grossly negligent.

Charlie   Don't you dare try to take a moral high ground with me, you little piece of cunt.

Aleksandr   She was informing to one of your fuck-holes. She was informing on a man called Andres Rebane. He's a stupid fuck who was trying to supply to massage parlours south of Earls Court. He thinks he's a big shot. He's a fucking pawn. He's working for a real evil fuck who calls himself the White Bird.

She knew Rebane from back in the day. He tried to sell her to me. I didn't want to pay him any money. She left him anyway because of the things he used to do to her and she came to work for me because she thought I was a fucking friendly face. I told her to tell the pigs about him. Get him off my fucking land. It was all she was good for. She met them once. Maybe twice. Told them fucking nothing. They did fuck all about it. She was a stupid useless cunt. Rebane found out. Must have got back to the White Bird. They sent me a DVD of what they had done to her. Do you want to see it?

Seven

DI **Charlie Lee**, *DS* **Ignatius Stone**. **Charlie**'s *office.*
They're watching the DVD.

Charlie   We should have known about her.

Ignatius *watches the DVD. Barely responds.*

Charlie   It should have been put on the database.

Ignatius *watches the DVD. Barely responds.*

Charlie   What's the point of even having a database if
people aren't going to flipping use it?

We don't know how many times he met her. We don't know
what kind of information they talked about.

Ignatius   It could have endangered her.

Charlie   I would say it kind of did endanger her, Iggy,
wouldn't you?

Ignatius *smiles. Doesn't answer. Watches the DVD.*

Charlie   But this is something else.

Ignatius   Yes.

Charlie   Klaus Brandt. Thirty-one years old. German
citizen since birth. Hamburg resident. One-hundred-per-cent
match from the German DNA database.

Ignatius   Handsome chap.

Charlie   There's no record anywhere of Andres Rebane.

Ignatius *watches the DVD.*

Charlie   Computer Operations giggled when I asked them
about the White Bird.

Ignatius *watches the DVD.*

Ignatius   I think he's Bavarian. Brandt. He's got a very
strong accent.

Charlie   How can you tell?

Ignatius   I used to live there.

Charlie   You did what?

Ignatius   I spent a year in Heidelberg when I was at university.

Charlie   No you didn't.

Ignatius   I studied Botany there.

Charlie   Why are you lying so, Ignatius?

Ignatius   I wrote my Master's thesis in their library.

Charlie   That's not true.

Ignatius   It's completely true. I lost my virginity in Germany too.

Charlie   Get away.

Ignatius   To a German, no less.

Charlie   You saucy bugger.

Ignatius   She was quite some years younger than me. Julia Breitner. She was a student. She was lovely.

Charlie *looks at him. Thinks.*

Looks at the film some more. Thinks.

Charlie   Do you still see her?

Ignatius *smiles. Shakes his head. Watches the DVD.*

Charlie   You could do.

Ignatius *glances at him, looking away from the DVD for the first time.*

Charlie   If we went back. Us two. Had a bit of a wander round Hamburg. Had a bit of a gander.

*It takes a while before **Ignatius** realises what he's suggesting.*

Ignatius   Are you being serious?

Charlie   Well, not about Julia Breitner, obviously. But I
think we should go ourselves and apprehend our suspect
rather than allowing anybody else to do it. That being what
we do. Apprehend our suspects.

Ignatius   We couldn't apprehend anybody, Charlie. Not in
Germany.

Charlie   We could get a European Arrest Warrant. We
could trace her family. We could get a Victim Impact Statement.
We wouldn't even need a translator.

Ignatius   I've not spoken German in fifteen years.

Charlie   You . . . racist.

Ignatius *chuckles.*

Charlie   We could find Rebane.

Ignatius   Do you think we could find the White Bird too?

Charlie   I'm being serious.

Ignatius   I've not actually seen anything like this before.

Charlie   No.

Ignatius   She's Caroline's age.

Charlie   You said.

Ignatius   How long would it take? To get the warrant? Just
out of interest.

Charlie   A very flipping long time.

Ignatius   I thought so.

Charlie   Months and months and months and months.

The two men look back at the screen.

Eight

DS **Ignatius Stone** *and* **Caroline Stone**. *Their flat.*

Caroline   What time's your flight?

Ignatius   Seven fifteen.

Caroline   From Heathrow?

Ignatius   From Heathrow.

Caroline   There's part of me that wants to get up in the morning and make you a big breakfast. But it's such a tiny little part of me that it doesn't really count. How are you feeling?

Ignatius   About what?

Caroline   About flying.

Ignatius   Almost completely terrified.

Caroline   Did you tell Charlie?

Ignatius   He knows. I've flown with him before.

Caroline   It's a very short flight, sweetheart.

Ignatius   It doesn't matter.

Caroline   Take an enormous amount of sleeping pills.

Ignatius   Good thinking.

Caroline   Drink a half-bottle of whisky.

Ignatius   Did you hear the seagulls last night?

Caroline   There's a nest of them above next-door's roof.

Ignatius   They kept me awake all night.

Caroline   They only just moved in. You'll get used to them. I wish I *was* coming with you.

Ignatius   You don't.

Caroline   Not to do your job with you. Just to, you know, hold your hand on the plane.

Are you going to get any free time?

Ignatius   I hope not.

Caroline   Haven't you still got lots of friends in Germany?

Ignatius   Not in Hamburg. It's very different from Heidelberg. It's practically a different country.

I'm really sorry I'm going.

Caroline   No you're not. Don't say that 'cause it's not true. You want to go.

Ignatius   Well, I want to find him. But I'd rather find him here. Not here literally. Not like in this flat. I feel shit about leaving you. I'm going to really miss you.

Caroline   Will you get to go to the Botanic Gardens?

Ignatius   I'd like to. I've no idea.

Caroline   Have they got anything interesting there?

Ignatius   They've an *Amorphophallus titanum*. A corpse flower. The largest unbranched inflorescence in the world. It stinks of rotting mammal flesh. It's Latin for 'giant misshapen penis'.

It would be fascinating.

Caroline   It's always funny to me.

Charlie   What is?

Caroline   The idea of you being in another country. The idea of you operating and carrying on and just being somewhere without me. I'm sorry – I'm being a bit weird, aren't I?

Ignatius *smiles at her.*

Caroline   Do you think you'll find him? The man on the film?

Ignatius   We might. We've been *very* lucky. We got a positive match on the German DNA database.

Caroline   Will you do me a favour?

Ignatius   Of course I will.

Caroline   Will you kick him in the face from me?

Ignatius   OK.

Caroline   Charlie wouldn't mind would he?

Ignatius   Not if I said it was from you he wouldn't.

Caroline   Kick him really hard.

Don't get depressed, will you?

Ignatius   I promise I won't.

Caroline   And don't drink too much.

Ignatius   OK.

Caroline   And don't smoke.

Ignatius   Smoke?

Caroline   Seriously, Iggy, I know you. As soon as you get to check in you'll be buying fags. Don't eat shit food.

Ignatius   OK.

Caroline   And don't get killed. I'd be so fucking cross if you got killed. I'd actually, I have to say, be generally pretty pissed off if you died before me for any reason.

Ignatius   Right.

Caroline   So just don't.

Ignatius   OK, I won't.

Caroline   Good.

Ignatius   I mean, I probably will.

Caroline   Don't.

Ignatius   Men tend to, don't they?

Caroline   Well, don't you then.

Ignatius   I'm fifteen years older than you.

Caroline   Well, just stop it then.

Ignatius   Stop what?

Caroline   Stop being fifteen years older than me, it's really inconsiderate.

You're funny.

Ignatius   Why?

Caroline   Your face.

Ignatius   What about my face?

Caroline   It's very, very serious all of a sudden.

© LSD Leonard Neumann (lsd-berlin.de)

Part Two: Hamburg

The money doesn't trickle down here. It trickles up. This whole city is built on the back of a Bulgarian teenager.

Das Geld sickert nicht nach hier unten. Es sickert nach oben. Die ganze Stadt ist gebaut auf dem Rücken eines bulgarischen Teenagers.

Siin ei liigu raha rikastelt vaestele. Siin liigub raha vaestelt rikastele. Terve see linn on Bulgaaria teismeliste selgade peale üles ehitatud.

One

The lobby of the Maritim Reichshoff Hotel, Hamburg. Eight p.m.
Detective **Steffen Dresner** *meets DS* **Ignatius Stone** *and DI*
Charlie Lee.

Steffen (*in English*)   My name's Detective Steffen Dresner. I
work for the sixth division, the organised crime division, of
the Hamburg District Police. Sub-division 5, the vice squad.
I'm in charge of a team of eleven detectives who work in the
St Georg area. Round here. Team 6.52. Our office is round
the corner at the Steindame. Herr Neuman told me he'd told
you about me.

Ignatius   Yes. He did. Sergeant Dresner. How lovely to
meet you.

Steffen   You speak German?

Ignatius   I used to more than I do now, but yes, I still do a
little.

Steffen   Right. Wow. Great. 'Cause I don't speak any
fucking English at all.

Ignatius   What?

Steffen   I don't.

Ignatius   No?

Steffen   I've been memorising that speech all morning.

Ignatius   You did it very well.

Steffen   Thank you. Thank fuck. Welcome to Hamburg.

Ignatius   Thank you very much.

Steffen   That's really fucking cool that you speak German.
Really fucking amazingly fucking useful actually.

Ignatius   Yes.

Steffen   You got here OK?

Ignatius   We did, thank you.

Steffen   How was your flight?

Ignatius   It was completely terrifying. We had a huge amount of turbulence.

Steffen   Shit, you speak really good German.

Ignatius   Thank you.

Steffen   Really fucking formal. It's really fluent.

Ignatius   Thank you.

Steffen   He speaks very good German, your colleague.

Charlie (*in English*)   What?

Steffen   And you don't.

Charlie (*in English*)   What?

Steffen   He doesn't.

Ignatius   Not a word.

Charlie (*in German*)   I'm sorry, I don't speak any Germany.

Steffen   Have they got you a translator?

Ignatius   We don't need one. I can translate for us.

Steffen   But you're not doing.

Ignatius   I will.

Steffen   Right.

Ignatius   The relevant bits.

Steffen   You used to live here, right?

Ignatius   Not here. In Heidelberg.

Steffen   Ha!

Ignatius   What?

Steffen   Fucking Heidleberg! When was that?

Ignatius   Twenty-five years ago.

Steffen   Fuck.

Ignatius   What?

Steffen   You're fucking old.

Ignatius   It was when I was a student.

Steffen   Groovy.

Ignatius   Studying Botany.

Steffen   Really?

Ignatius   Yes.

Steffen   Fucking flowers?

Ignatius   –

Charlie (*in English*)   What's he saying?

Ignatius (*in English*)   He's asking me about my student days.

Charlie (*in English*)   Great.

Steffen   It's changed, Germany, in the last twenty-five years.

Ignatius   I'm sure it has.

Steffen   This city's got a lot fucking richer.

Ignatius   Terrific.

Steffen   We're getting a new Philharmonic Concert Hall.

Ignatius   A Philharmonic Concert Hall?

Steffen   It's where all our fucking money's going. Got no money for any ambulances any more. No money for any fucking new cars for the Kriminal Polizei. No money for cleaning the streets or to pay for all the fucking millions of fucking Turkish fucking Arab fuck-holes who can't stop heading fucking northwards but we're getting a really exciting Philharmonic Concert Hall.

Ignatius   Lovely.

Steffen   I love Philharmonic concerts, me. I'm fucking mad for them. Do you think you'll get much free time?

Ignatius   I doubt it.

Steffen   We could try and arrange some for you. Maybe you could watch a Philharmonic concert.

Ignatius (*in English*)   They're going to try to arrange some free time for us.

Charlie (*in English*)   Super.

Ignatius (*in English*)   He really likes symphonies.

Charlie (*in English*)   Great. Me too.

Steffen   Is there anything you'd particularly like to do?

Ignatius   To do?

Steffen   While you're here in Hamburg. With your free time.

Ignatius   I was expecting to be working for most of the time we were here.

Steffen   Fuck yes, of course, but . . .

Ignatius   That's what we're here for.

Steffen   I know that.

Ignatius   Not for a weekend break.

Steffen   No. Sure. But. There may be a bit of time free and I was just fucking asking if you had, you know, hopes or fucking plans or anything.

Beat.

You could go to the Beatles-Platz.

Ignatius   The what?

Steffen   It's a memorial square for the fucking Beatles near the Kaiserkellar. There are some really fucking stupid statues there. English people fucking love it. I do too. I fucking love The Beatles. Shit. They were great.

How's your room?

Ignatius   It's fine.

Steffen   I like this hotel.

Ignatius   I like it too.

Steffen   They do a great breakfast here.

Ignatius   Terrific. (*In English.*) They do a great breakfast, he says.

Charlie (*in English*)   Magic.

Steffen   I like this lobby too. I like hotels as a rule. I spend a lot of time in hotels. I always find them quite sexy.

Ignatius   Sexy?

Steffen   Don't you?

Ignatius   I'm not sure. I always feel a bit like a dog in a new room.

Steffen   A dog?

Ignatius   I always have the inclination to sniff around them.

Steffen   They have a remarkable range of whisky in the bar.

Ignatius   Lovely.

Steffen   Really. Hundreds of different bottles of whisky.

Ignatius   Great.

Steffen   Should I tell you a little bit more about what the fuck I'm doing here?

Ignatius   You could do.

Steffen   So. Herr Neuman asked me to help you because the few leads he's got on your case would tend to suggest that this is the area of the city that's most worthy of investigation. And I know this area. I mean, I really know it. Like you wouldn't fucking believe. Seriously. You can ask me fucking anything. I'll fucking know the answer.

Ignatius (*in English*)   Great. Detective Dresner is an expert in this part of the city. This is the part of the city they think we'll find Brandt and Rebane.

Charlie (*in English*)   Good.

Steffen   We've never heard of Andres Rebane. We've got no record of him at all. He's on no computers in either the whole of Hamburg or across the German network.

Pause.

Ignatius (*in English*)   They've never heard of Andres Rebane. They've got no record of him at all. He's on no computers in either the whole of Hamburg or across the German network.

Charlie (*in English*)   Good Lord. That's a tad – what? Disappointing?

Ignatius   He's a little disappointed. I am too I have to say.

Steffen   Yes. We've had very few Russians here. They tend to work the Reeperbahn. We've had some. Not many. And none of them called Andres Rebane. And we've never had Estonians. We've not met Estonians. We've not arrested Estonians. We've never charged Estonians. There are no fucking Estonians working vice on the streets of St Georg. We thought maybe they didn't work the streets. Maybe they worked out of the hotels or the flats around here and advertised in the *Morning Post*. It's amazing what people advertise in the *Morning Post* here. So far we've found nothing. Do you want to translate that?

Ignatius (*in English*)   They have very few Russians working in vice in St Georg and as far as he can tell no Estonians.

Steffen   And Klaus Brandt has completely disappeared. Which is probably also bad news for you, no?

Ignatius   Yes, it is rather. (*In English.*) Brandt's disappeared too.

Steffen   He's not been on our records for eighteen months. He's not moved to St Pauli. He's not been arrested anywhere. He's not registered any calls on the phone that we had for him or withdrawn or deposited any money into the accounts of his we had access to. He's left.

Ignatius   Right.

Steffen   We think. We're not sure. We're still looking. But we think he's left.

Charlie (*in English*)   What's that?

Ignatius (*in English*)   He's just saying the same thing again but using more words.

Charlie (*in English*)   I really like it when people do that.

Ignatius   Herr Neuman told us you had a record of Vera Petrova. That she might have lived in St Georg for a while.

Steffen   Yes, we do. We did. She did, I think. Yes. We had her DNA. She was taken in for Actual Bodily Harm in January 2009. She attacked another street worker on Danzigerstrasse. Cut her face open with a beer bottle. Kristina Suvi. Petrova was registered as actually living at the same address as Suvi. They were flatmates.

Ignatius (*in English*)   They took her DNA after she smashed a beer bottle into her flatmate's face.

Steffen   We've not seen her since.

Ignatius (*in English*)   They've lost her too.

Steffen   Did he not tell you any of this?

Ignatius   No.

Steffen   Did nobody tell you this before you came here?

Ignatius   No.

Steffen   I imagine it's a bit annoying, isn't it?

Ignatius   It is a little.

Steffen   I imagine it makes you feel like you're fucking completely wasting you're fucking time here a bit, no?

Ignatius   A little. Maybe. Not really.

Steffen   We've got the photograph of your man outside the pub in West London. We've been showing that around a bit.

We've got all the CCTV from the garage and the theatre and those hotels that co-operate and the bars on the Steindame and the Lange Reiher for the past six months. We can use them if we need to but, you know, that's a lot of fucking film, yes? We're talking to Eleanor. On the corner. She's been here forty-two years. She told us she'll fucking talk to us if one of her fucking colleagues has had her fucking head cut off. She's fucking crazy but she'll talk to us about that. Hates cops. Fucks a few of them. Not many. Not as much as she used to.

Pause.

Ignatius (*in English*)   They're going to keep checking.

Steffen   But we did find a distributor for White Bird Merchants.

Ignatius (*in English*)   They found a distributor for White Bird Merchants.

Steffen   A Russian-born film director called Georg Kohler who operates out of an office near Davidstrasse in St Pauli. Some of my colleagues in 6.51 know Kohler. They've known him for years. I've seen some of his work. We could go and see him.

Ignatius (*in English*)   He's suggesting going to pay him a call.

Charlie (*in English*)   I'd rather go to the Philharmonic Concert Hall if that's OK.

Ignatius   He thinks that's a terrific idea. We'd love to come with you.

Steffen   Excellent. I was going over to see him tomorrow morning. About ten o'clock. I'll collect you.

Ignatius   Do.

Steffen   I work all the time.

Ignatius   What?

Steffen   I do. I work all the time. Officially I'm eight-to-four but fuck that, eh? I work all the time. What else is there to do?

Charlie   Iggy.

Ignatius   Charlie.

Charlie (*in English*)   Ask him if he was contacted before.

Ignatius   Were you contacted before?

Steffen   Before?

Ignatius   By British police looking for Rebane?

Steffen   I don't think so. I don't have any recollection.
Of course I'll check the database. That's easy to do. But no.
No. No. Not as far as I can remember. And I remember
fucking everything.

Two

The bar at the Reichshoff. That night. **Ignatius** *and* **Charlie**
address one another in English.

Charlie   If I wasn't such an innately optimistic man I'd
suggest that this is a complete waste of time. Us being here.

Ignatius   Yeah.

Charlie   I'd propose that we go back.

Ignatius   Yeah.

Charlie   And perhaps then we could come back when
they've actually got the fucker.

Ignatius   Yeah.

Charlie   I can't understand a word anybody's actually
saying to me. It's all a huge babble. It makes me feel
uncharacteristically lonely.

Would you like another?

Ignatius   Yeah.

Charlie   I do like an island malt.

Ignatius   Me too.

Charlie   Will you do me a favour?

Ignatius   Of course I will.

Charlie   Will you translate more for me?

Ignatius   More?

Charlie   More of what Steffen's saying. More of what Neuman's saying. More of what everybody's saying.

Ignatius   I translate the relevant bits.

Charlie   You need to translate the completely irrelevant bits too.

Ignatius   I'll do my best.

Charlie   You've no idea what it's like. It's completely disorientating.

Three

The doorway of **Ignatius Stone***'s hotel room.* **Stephanie Friedmann** *is standing there.*

Stephanie   I'm sorry.

Ignatius   What for?

Stephanie   For bothering you.

Ignatius   Can I help you?

Stephanie   I thought I heard screaming coming from your room.

Ignatius   –

Stephanie   I'm sorry, you must think I'm a bit . . . Sorry. I couldn't sleep. I thought I heard somebody screaming and I got out of my room and I followed it. It sounded like it was coming from inside here.

Ignatius I see. Oh dear.

Stephanie There wasn't anybody screaming in here, was there?

Ignatius No. No there wasn't, no. I'm sorry.

Stephanie I hope I didn't wake you up.

Ignatius No. You didn't, no. I wasn't asleep.

Stephanie Right, good. That's. That's good then. That's a relief.

Ignatius There are seagulls on the roof of the hotel. They were keeping me awake. It's like they're following me.

Stephanie Really?

Ignatius Well no, not really. Clearly not. This is a port city. Of course there are seagulls here. It's just that there are seagulls nesting near my home in London, which is more unusual. It was just a little joke.

Stephanie You speak very good German.

Ignatius Thank you.

Stephanie Where did you learn to speak such good German?

Ignatius I lived in Heidelberg for a while. When you live in a country then you really get to learn the language.

Stephanie I wouldn't know that. I've never lived anywhere other than Hamburg.

Ignatius Right.

Stephanie Yes.

Ignatius Well. I hear Hamburg's a great city.

Stephanie It is. What are you doing here?

Ignatius What?

Stephanie What are you doing here, in Hamburg?

Ignatius   Is that any of your business?

Stephanie   I'm sorry. I should go.

Ignatius   No. I'm sorry. That was – I didn't mean to seem –
I'm being terribly rude.

Stephanie   You're not.

Ignatius   I am. I'm tired. That's no excuse. I've had rather
a bad day. That's no excuse either.

Stephanie   Why was your day bad?

Ignatius   Oh. I just. I don't really like flying.

Stephanie   No?

Ignatius   No. I'm working.

Stephanie   What work are you doing?

Ignatius   I'm a policeman. I'm a detective.

Stephanie   Are you investigating a terrible crime?

Ignatius *smiles.*

Stephanie   Gosh. How exciting.

Funny.

Ignatius   What?

Stephanie   The signs saying which way the room numbers go.

Ignatius   What about them?

Stephanie   Where are they actually?

Ignatius   I don't know.

Stephanie   No. I'll find them.

Ignatius   Which room number are you in?

Stephanie   327. I'm Stephanie.

Ignatius   Right. Sorry. I'm Ignatius.

Stephanie   Hello, Ignatius.

Ignatius   Hi, Stephanie.

Stephanie   Hi.

I'm going to leave you. I'll leave you to – you know. Go to sleep.

Ignatius   Thank you.

Stephanie   Would you like to have breakfast with me tomorrow?

Ignatius   Er.

Stephanie   Tomorrow morning.

Ignatius   I think I'll probably be having breakfast with my colleague.

Stephanie   OK.

Ignatius   We're here together.

Stephanie   That's a pity.

Ignatius   You could come and join us.

Stephanie   I don't think so.

Ignatius   You could.

Stephanie   I like Englishmen.

Ignatius   Well, that's good.

Stephanie   You don't look very English.

Ignatius   No.

Stephanie   You don't look like Paul McCartney at all.

Ignatius   What? No. I don't think I do either.

Stephanie   You don't look like Hugh Grant.

Ignatius   No.

Stephanie   You don't look like David Beckham.

Four

The breakfast room of the Reichshoff. **Ignatius Stone** *and* **Charlie Lee** *are joined by* **Steffen Dresner**.

Steffen   Good morning.

Ignatius   Good morning.

Steffen   Good morning.

Charlie   Good morning.

Steffen   You sleep OK?

Ignatius   OK. Thank you. Not bad. (*In English.*) He's asking how we slept.

Charlie (*in English*)   Great. Like a happy sleeping little flipping angel.

Steffen   Room OK?

Ignatius   Fine, yes. Thank you. (*In English.*) You happy with the room?

Charlie (*in English*)   I think it's the best hotel room I've ever seen in my life.

Ignatius   Yeah. He's happy too.

Steffen   Good view?

Ignatius   There's a view of the middle of the hotel. The air vents. The fire escapes. I can't figure out the shape of the corridors.

Steffen   No.

Ignatius   It's like they twist around each other.

Steffen   They do.

Charlie (*in English*)   What was that?

Ignatius (*in English*)   We were just talking about the weird shape of the corridors.

Charlie (*in English*)   It sounded more pressing than that.

Ignatius (*in English*)   It wasn't.

Charlie (*in English*)   No. Good. Carry on.

Ignatius   Are you just starting?

Steffen   What?

Ignatius   Your shift, is it just starting?

Steffen   No.

Ignatius   No?

Steffen   I've been on all night.

Ignatius (*in English*)   He's been working all night. (*In German.*) You don't look tired.

Charlie (*in English*)   He doesn't look very tired.

Ignatius   What were you working on?

Steffen   Oh. You know. The world. How's your coffee?

Ignatius   Lovely.

Steffen   I told you it was a fucking good place to have fucking breakfast, didn't I?

Ignatius   You did, yes.

Steffen   I was fucking right as well. You had the muesli?

Ignatius   Yes, I did.

Steffen   The yoghurt muesli?

Ignatius   Yes.

Steffen   Did you put the extra cherry on it?

Ignatius   I didn't, no.

Steffen   You fucking should have done. It's fucking fantastic. You should get some more. That's the fucking thing with a fucking buffet. You can have as much as you want. You could get me some. You could get me my fucking lunch.

Ignatius (*in English*)   He's terribly excited about the cherry muesli and wants us to steal his lunch from the buffet.

Charlie (*in English*)   Brilliant.

Steffen   So. I checked for previous enquiries from the UK.

Ignatius (*in English*)   He checked for previous enquiries from the UK.

Steffen   Fucking nothing.

Ignatius (*in English*)   Nothing.

Steffen   We've found some Lithuanians.

Ignatius (*in English*)   They've found some Lithuanians.

Steffen   We're talking to them about Rebane and Petrov. They've not said anything. Denied all fucking, what? Knowledge? Denied all knowledge. We'll keep pestering them. They'll fucking crack in the end. They'll get really fucking annoyed. Especially if she was fucking grassing, this Petrov girl.

Ignatius   Grassing?

Steffen   Vera Petrova?

Ignatius   Who told you that?

Steffen   Wasn't she?

Ignatius   Who told you that she was grassing?

Steffen   I knew she fucking was. You should see your fucking face, Sergeant Stone. It's fucking funny. Course she was fucking grassing. Why the fuck else would you fucking do some fucking fucked-up shit like that if she wasn't fucking grassing?

And Eleanor's seen Kristina Suvi. A few weeks ago. So. She's around. She's here. We'll find her.

Ignatius (*in English*)   A local informant has seen Kristina Suvi.

Charlie (*in English*)   Ace!

Steffen   And look at this. These are stills from the same batch of films you sent us. The StudentSexParties films. Vera, yes? Now look at the symbol on the menu above the television. That's a German hotel. That's a Hamburg hotel. The Marine Hotel behind the station. That film was made here. Kohler must have made it.

Ignatius   In Hamburg?

Steffen   Not in Russia at all. Russian models. Made in Hamburg.

Ignatius (*in English*)   This hotel is in Hamburg, not Moscow. He thinks Kohler definitely made it.

Charlie (*in English*)   Crumbs.

Steffen   And do you know who this is? This girl here with Vera. She's Kristina Suvi.

Ignatius (*in English*)   This is Kristina Suvi.

Charlie (*in English*)   But they seem to be getting on so well.

Steffen   And then wait. This is from the same film. It's a different excerpt from another website but it's the same film. And look at this boy. This one on the right with the beer. Recognise him?

Ignatius   Is that Brandt?

Steffen   We think so.

Ignatius (*in English*)   This rather handsomely proportioned young man is Brandt.

Charlie (*in English*)   Well, he's got nothing to be ashamed of, has he?

Steffen   He speaks. In the film he speaks.

Ignatius (*in English*)   He speaks in the film.

Charlie (*in English*)   Well, that's clever.

Steffen   He's Bavarian.

Five

The offices of **Georg Kohler**. **Steffen**, **Ignatius** *and* **Charlie**
are there to interview him.

Steffen   Is your name Georg Kohler?

Georg   What?

Steffen   Is your name Georg Kohler?

Georg   I don't know who you're talking about.

Steffen   Fuck this.

He grabs his hair and slaps him hard across the face.

Is your name Georg Kohler?

Georg   Yes. Yes. I'm Georg Kohler. Yes.

Steffen   See. I knew that. They knew that. You knew that
we all knew that so why did you have to make it fucking
difficult for yourself? Christ. I'm embarrassed now. You've
embarrassed me in front of my British colleagues. What the
fuck did you do that for?

Georg   You hit me.

Steffen   No I didn't.

Georg   You fucking hit me.

Steffen   I didn't touch you. Shut the fuck up, you snivelling
fuck-ball.

Georg   You saw him. You saw him hit me, didn't you?

Charlie (*in German*)   I'm sorry I don't speak any Germany.

Georg   He hit me.

Charlie (*in English*)   What's he saying?

Ignatius (*in English*)   He seems to be making the allegation
that Detective Dresner assaulted him.

Charlie (*in English*)   No?

Ignatius (*in English*)   It's what he's saying.

Charlie (*in English*)   Mr Kohler, we want to talk to you with regards to a murder that was committed in London in May.

Ignatius   Mr Kohler we want to talk to you with regards to a murder that was committed in London in May.

Georg   A murder?

Ignatius   That's right. We think one of your models was murdered.

Georg   What models? I don't understand what you mean by 'one of my models'. I don't own any models.

Steffen   Is it me or is he really annoying?

Ignatius   He is a little annoying.

Steffen   Should I shut him up?

Ignatius   What?

Steffen   Here.

He punches him hard in the face.

Ah, that actually hurt my fist.

He punches him again.

It stings a bit. Have you got any water, Mr Kohler. I could do with running my hand under some water. If you want to, you can have a go. Look at him.

Ignatius   He's not done anything.

Steffen   What?

Ignatius   I think you over-reacted. He's not really done anything.

Steffen   No?

Last time we took him in I saw his computer. Do you know what a ten-year-old girl looks like with a sixty-year-old's cock in her mouth?

He leaves.

Charlie (*in English*)   Crikey.

Ignatius (*in English*)   He's got one or two issues with some of the films that Mr Kohler makes.

Charlie (*in English*)   Ah! I wondered what it was. Is this where you make your films?

Ignatius   Is this where you make your films?

Georg   Yes.

Charlie (*in English*)   All of them?

Ignatius   All of them?

Georg   Yes.

Charlie (*in English*)   It smells fantastic.

Ignatius (*in English*)   It does smell striking, doesn't it?

Charlie (*in English*)   It smells like rubber. And what? Shit?

Ignatius (*in English*)   Yes. Kind of like shit.

Steffen *comes back with a towel over his hand.*

Charlie (*in English*)   There was a series of films you distributed over the last two years called StudentSexParties. Do you remember those, Mr Kohler?

Ignatius   There was a series of films you distributed over the last two years called StudentSexParties. Do you remember those Mr Kohler?

Mr Kohler, do you remember those films?

Steffen   Do you want me to hit you fucking properly, you fucking midget?

Georg   Yes. I remember those films.

Ignatius (*in English*)   He remembers them.

Charlie (*in English*)   Great. Did you direct those films, Mr Kohler, or did you just distribute them?

Georg   What?

Ignatius   Did you direct those films, Mr Kohler, or did you just distribute them?

Georg   I don't know what you're talking about.

Steffen   Mr Kohler, you didn't just buy those films from a foreign producer, did you? You directed them, didn't you, Mr Kohler? Didn't you, Mr Kohler?

Georg   That's not illegal.

Steffen   No, I fucking know it's not illegal. you fucking cunt-faced shit.

Georg   It's not illegal to make a film.

Ignatius (*in English*)   He's claiming that the films weren't illegal.

Steffen   I'm not saying that. Am I saying that?

Ignatius   I'm fairly certain that you're not saying that, I have to say.

Georg   It's not illegal to make money.

Steffen   Clearly. Fuck. I'm just gonna hit him. Is that all right? I'm just gonna hit him again.

Georg   Don't.

Steffen   What?

Georg   Don't hit me any more.

Ignatius (*in English*)   He asked him to not hit him any more.

Georg   Yes. I directed those films. Yes.

Ignatius (*in English*)   He directed the films.

Charlie (*in English*)   Did you know this girl?

Ignatius   Did you know this girl?

They show him a photograph.

Georg   That's Vera Kukk.

A skinny, little, hungry bit of cunt.

Charlie *shows him a photograph from the crime scene.*

Ignatius   Is this her?

Georg   Fuck.

Ignatius   Is this her, Georg?

Georg   What happened to her?

Steffen   What does it fucking look like, you snivelling fuck-cake?

Ignatius   Is this her in the photograph, Mr Kohler?

Georg   I think so, yes.

Ignatius   Do you know where she lived when you were working with her?

Georg   Where she lived?

Ignatius   Vera Kukk, as you call her – do you know where she was living when you made your films with her?

Georg   No. No. No. I don't. I'm sorry.

Ignatius   When was the last time you made a film with her, Mr Kohler?

Georg   Two years ago. Maybe. Eighteen months ago.

Ignatius   And this girl?

Georg   That's Kristina Suvi. She's a stupid cunt.

Charlie (*in English*)   Ask him if he recognises Klaus Brandt.

Ignatius   Do you know this man?

Georg   Him? The blond one?

Ignatius   Yes.

Georg   Yes. Of course I know him. He's one of the lead actors. He worked with the producers all the time. Male actors often do. He did some of the logistics. Helped hire the cameraman. Shot it himself sometimes. Found the rooms. Rented them. He pimps the girls.

Ignatius   Pimps them?

Georg   Yeah.

Ignatius   All of them?

Georg   What, yes, all of them.

Ignatius   Did he own Vera?

Georg   Yes. he owned all of them.

Steffen   What about Kristina Suvi?

Georg   Are you two fucking deaf?

Ignatius (*in English*)   He knew him well. He was the main producer of the films. He arranged everything. He sold them directly to Shumaker. He pimped the girls as well. Including Vera and Kristina Suvi.

Charlie (*in English*)   So the likelihood is that if we find Suvi –

Ignatius (*in English*)   Then we find Brandt.

Steffen   You are one pair of lucky, lucky fucks.

Charlie (*in English*)   Was Brandt employed by a man called Andres Rebane?

Ignatius   Was Brandt employed by a man called Andres Rebane?

Georg   I don't know. I only met Brandt.

Charlie (*in English*)   Have you ever heard the name Andres Rebane?

Ignatius   Have you ever heard the name Andres Rebane?

Georg   I don't think so, no.

Charlie (*in English*)   Why is the film company who made these films called White Bird Merchants?

Ignatius   Why is the film company called White Bird Merchants?

Georg   I have no idea.

Ignatius (*in English*)   He doesn't know.

Charlie (*in English*)   Has he ever heard of a man called the White Bird?

Ignatius   Have you ever heard of a man called the White Bird?

Steffen *can't stop himself from giggling slightly.* **Georg** *giggles too a bit.*

Steffen   Is that a serious question?

Ignatius   Have you ever heard of a man called the White Bird?

Georg   No. I haven't. No.

Ignatius (*in English*)   He hasn't. No.

Steffen   That's about the funniest question I've ever heard anybody ask with a straight face.

He sings a refrain from the popular song. **Georg** *chuckles at this a little.*

Charlie   Is he completely sure about that?

Ignatius   Are you completely sure about that?

Georg   Totally.

Ignatius   Totally.

Charlie   Is he aware about how much trouble he'll be in if he's lying?

Ignatius   Are you aware of how much trouble you'll be in if you're lying?

Six

The breakfast room at the Reichshof. **Ignatius**, **Charlie** *and* **Stephanie**.

Stephanie   I can't imagine you studying flowers.

Ignatius   I like flowers.

Stephanie   Why?

Ignatius   I like how they're robust and delicate at the same time. They make me feel hopeful. I like the way they smell. I like nature. I don't see enough of it any more.

Charlie (*in English*)   What did you say then?

Ignatius (*in English*)   You really don't want to know.

Charlie (*in English*)   You dirty old dog.

Stephanie   Do you mind me asking him questions like this?

Charlie   I'm sorry, I don't speak any Germany.

She looks at **Charlie**. *Doesn't know what to say. Turns back to* **Ignatius**.

Ignatius (*in English*)   She's asking you if you mind her asking me questions like this.

Charlie (*in English*)   Is she?

Ignatius (*in English*)   Yes, she is.

Charlie *chuckles.*

Charlie (*in English*)   No. No. No. Not at all. You carry on.

Ignatius   He doesn't mind at all. He's enjoying eating an enormous breakfast.

Stephanie   Are you a very good detective?

Ignatius   I don't know.

Stephanie   Are you a little bit maverick?

Ignatius   Not maverick, no.

Stephanie   Do you eat lots of chocolate doughnuts and chain-smoke cigarettes and drink lots and lots of coffee and whisky?

Ignatius   Not really I don't.

Stephanie   Do you fight people all the time and really beat the life out of them?

Ignatius   No.

Stephanie   I bet you could, though. I'd love to see that. Have you ever killed anybody?

Ignatius   No. I haven't. No.

Stephanie   Are you lying? I bet you're lying to protect me from the terrible truth.

Charlie (*in English*)   What's she asking you now?

Ignatius (*in English*)   She's asking me about my procedural behaviour.

Charlie (*in English*)   I bet she flipping is.

Stephanie   What does your wife do?

Ignatius   She's a writer. She writes local travel journalism. She's fifteen years younger than me.

Stephanie   That must be rather bracing, isn't it?

Ignatius   Bracing?

Stephanie   Does she keep you young?

Ignatius   I don't – Yes. I'm not sure.

Stephanie   Do you mind?

Ignatius   What?

Stephanie   If I see your hand.

Ignatius   What?

Stephanie   Can I just see it?

Ignatius   My hand?

Stephanie   Yes.

Ignatius   OK.

Charlie (*in English*)   Aye Karumba!.

Stephanie   I thought so.

Ignatius   What?

Charlie (*in English*)   Is she reading your palm?

Ignatius (*in English*)   I've no idea.

Stephanie   You have good hands.

Charlie (*in English*)   Tell her you're a Virgo.

Stephanie   They're very big. You've got long fingers. Does that feel nice?

Charlie (*in English*)   He's a Virgo, you know?

Stephanie   You'll find him.

Ignatius   Who?

Stephanie   The man you're looking for. You really want to, don't you?

You haven't slept in days and days, have you? It's because of what you see when you close your eyes. He won't be where you think he'll be. He'll be in the last place you think of looking.

Seven

Kristina Suvi's *flat*. **Kristina, Ignatius, Michael** *and* **Steffen**.

Steffen   I promise you that you have absolutely nothing to be frightened of.

Kristina   I know that.

Steffen   Eleanor's downstairs. She's not going to let anybody come up. She promised me. She's nice, Eleanor, isn't she?

Kristina   Yeah.

Steffen   Do you know how long I've known her?

Kristina   No.

Steffen   Longer than you think I have, I bet. This is Charlie.

Charlie   Hello.

Kristina   Hello.

Steffen   Charlie's a bit of a fucking idiot. He can't speak a word of German. We could say fucking anything we wanted to and he wouldn't understand a word we've said.

Kristina   Really?

Steffen   Really.

Kristina   Ha.

Steffen   Like did you know his penis is really tiny and it looks like a mouse's penis?

Kristina   No.

Steffen   It's true.

Kristina   I bet it's true. It looks true. You can tell it to look at him.

What about him?

Steffen   This is Iggy.

Ignatius   And I speak fairly decent German so you should probably be slightly more cautious about what you say around me.

Kristina   OK.

Ignatius   But I promise you I won't tell Charlie what you said.

Kristina   OK.

Steffen   How did you hurt your face, Kristina? You don't need to tell us that if you don't want to.

Ignatius   We're not here to talk to you.

Steffen   Well, we are. We do want to talk to you. But all we want to do is to talk to you.

But you know that, don't you?

We're really glad you called us.

Was it Klaus Brandt who did this to your face?

Kristina   Eleanor told me you were looking for him.

Ignatius   Yeah.

Kristina   She smells strange nowadays, have you noticed that?

Steffen   I don't think I have, no. I've not really smelt her much.

Kristina   I've got a great sense of smell me.

Steffen   Have you?

Kristina   It's my most striking quality. I can smell anything. Do you want to test me?

Ignatius (*in English*)   She's boasting about her remarkable sense of smell and inviting us to test it.

Kristina   I can smell the cherry muesli that the tiny-dicked English cop had for breakfast, for example.

Steffen   Ha! Ask him what he had for breakfast.

Ignatius   He had the cherry muesli. I was with him.

Kristina   See?

Steffen   That's fucking amazing.

Charlie (*in English*)   Yes?

Ignatius (*in English*)   He's softening her with small talk.

Charlie (*in English*)   That's what it looked like from here. Sometimes you can just tell. You don't even need to know the words.

Kristina   And I can smell exactly what you're made up of.

Ignatius   What do you mean?

Kristina   It doesn't matter. Has Klaus done something very bad?

Steffen   Well. We don't know that.

Kristina   Right.

Ignatius   Something bad has happened, though.

Steffen   Kristina, do you remember Vera Petrova?

Kristina   Vera?

Ignatius   She worked in Hamburg for a short time.

Kristina   Yes. Of course I remember Vera. I lived with Vera. Why would I not remember her?

Ignatius   One time you and she had a bit of a falling out, didn't you?

Kristina   She smashed a bottle into my fucking face.

Ignatius   Yeah. I heard that. Why was that, Kristina?

Kristina   What?

Ignatius   Why did she attack you? (*In English.*) I'm asking her about Vera attacking her. She's gone suddenly quite quiet.

Charlie (*in English*)   Now, you see, I noticed that as well.

Ignatius   You made some films with her and Klaus and Georg Kohler. Do you remember Georg Kohler, Kristina?

Kristina   Yes.

Ignatius   Did you make those films in Hamburg, Kristina?

Kristina   Yes. It was a couple of years ago. It was at the Marine.

Ignatius   Yeah.

Kristina   What's happened to her? Is she OK?

Steffen   She's not, I'm afraid, Kristina. No.

Kristina   Right. Is she dead?

Fuck. That's fucking shit, isn't it? That's a real fucking pain.

She was young too, wasn't she?

Ignatius   She was twenty-eight.

Kristina   Oh shit. I thought she was younger than that. I thought she was my age.

Ignatius   No. She was twenty-eight.

Kristina   That's not too young then, is it?

Fuck. Do you think, you don't think, do you think Klaus . . .

No. Not Klaus. He wouldn't do that. What a stupid mistake! No. He's. He wouldn't have it in him.

Ignatius   We know that.

Kristina   There's no fucking way.

Steffen   We know that, Kristina. We just think he might know some people who might know some people who might have been involved in what happened to her. We just want to ask him some questions. OK? Is that OK, Kristina?

Ignatius   Have you been working all day?

What time did you start?

Kristina   Six.

Ignatius   Six this morning?

What time will you finish, do you think?

Kristina   Midnight.

Ignatius   A long shift.

Kristina   Yeah.

Steffen   Eleanor told us about Silbie and – Eduardo, is it?

Kristina   Yeah.

Steffen   How old are they?

Kristina   Four and six.

Ignatius   Good ages.

Kristina *starts tapping her foot as she talks.*

Kristina   Yeah. They're lovely. Silbie's like me. She's a real chatterbox. Eduardo is brilliant. He's so clever. He's a brilliant artist. He's grumpy though. He has an artistic temperament.

Steffen   Eleanor says you're not allowed to see them any more.

Kristina   I am. She must have got that wrong.

Ignatius   Why aren't you allowed to see them any more?

Kristina   I am. She doesn't know what she's talking about.

Charlie (*in English*)   Why's she tapping her foot like that?

Ignatius (*in English*)   Because she's lying about how much she sees her children.

Charlie   Yeah.

She stops tapping her foot.

Ignatius   Have you ever heard of a man called Andres Rebane, Kristina?

Kristina   No.

Ignatius   No. Did you ever hear that name when you were living in Russia?

Kristina   No.

Ignatius   Did you have many dealings with White Bird Merchants?

Kristina   I only worked with Georg. I never met the producers.

Ignatius (*in English*)   She never met the producers from White Bird Merchants.

Charlie (*in English*)   I kind of guessed she wouldn't have done. Ask her if she's ever heard of a man who calls himself the White Bird.

Ignatius   Have you ever heard of a man who calls himself the White Bird?

Steffen *giggles again.* **Kristina** *can't help but join in. They sing a bit of the song together.*

Kristina   No. I've not. I mean that's a pretty fucking stupid name. I've met a lot of men with a lot of stupid names but nobody with a name quite as stupid as that. Is he a fucking super-hero or something?

Steffen *enjoys her joke. Giggles more. Tries to control it.*

Ignatius (*in English*)   Apparently not. (*In German again.*) Whereabouts in Russia are you from?

Kristina   From the West. From Narva.

Ignatius   Is Narva in Russia?

Kristina   Kind of. It's kind of Russia. Kind of Estonia.

Ignatius   Yeah.

Kristina   It's on the border.

Ignatius (*in English*)   She's from Estonia.

Charlie (*in English*)   Bingo. Ask her where he is.

Ignatius   Where is he, Kristina? Where's Klaus?

She starts tapping her foot again.

Kristina   I don't know.

Ignatius (*in English*)   She doesn't know.

Charlie (*in English*)   When was the last time she saw him?

Ignatius   When was the last time you saw him?

Kristina   Weeks ago.

Ignatius (*in English*)   She's not seen him for weeks.

Charlie (*in English*)   And oh crikey, look at her foot! Now there's a surprise!

Ignatius   Kristina, don't lie. When you lie you keep tapping your foot – did you know that?

She stops.

When was the last time you saw him, Kristina?

Steffen   Tell him, Kristina.

Kristina   This morning.

Ignatius (*in English*)   She saw him this morning.

Ignatius   Is he your boyfriend?

Kristina   Yes, he is.

Steffen   Is he?

Kristina   Yeah.

Steffen   That's good. Does he live here?

Kristina   Does it look like he lives here?

Steffen   When's he coming back?

Kristina   He didn't say.

Ignatius (*in English*)   She says he didn't say when he's coming back.

Charlie (*in English*)   She's lying.

Steffen   Really, didn't he?

Kristina   Really.

Charlie   Well. We'll wait for him, I think. If that's OK with you.

Ignatius   We'll wait for him.

Kristina   He might be away a long time.

Steffen   We know that.

Ignatius (*in English*)   She says he might be away a long time.

Charlie (*in English*)   Oh, all night probably. We can wait in the hotel. Keep watching.

Kristina   He might be away all night.

Ignatius   Yeah.

Kristina   He might be away for days.

Ignatius   Yeah.

Eight

The hotel bar. **Steffen** *and* **Ignatius**.

Steffen   He's a funny fucker, isn't he?

Ignatius   I don't know what you mean.

Steffen   His questions are fucking funny. He's like Columbo. He makes me laugh. I like him a fucking lot. 'I'm sorry I don't speak any Germany.' Dick.

Ignatius   He likes you too.

Steffen   I can tell that. How long have you worked with him?

Ignatius   Seven years.

Steffen   You make a good team, yeah?

Ignatius   I think so.

Steffen   Do you never think you'd be better off without him?

Ignatius   No. I don't. No.

Steffen   Why does he keep going on about the White Bird?

Ignatius   It's just a name we heard in London. We think it's worth investigating.

Steffen   Yeah. Sounds it. London. Fucking crazy city, yeah? Do all the bad guys have names like that in London?

Ignatius *smiles, doesn't answer.*

Steffen   Do you think she'll tell him we've found him before we get to him?

Ignatius   Maybe.

Steffen   Her face.

Ignatius   Yeah.

Steffen   Fucking women, man. Fuck. Why do they?

Ignatius   What?

Steffen   Fucking put up with me? How old do you think she was?

Ignatius   Twenty-one. Twenty-two. Young.

Steffen   Yeah. Even by your standards, Detective Stone, eh?

Ignatius   I'm sorry?

Steffen   I'm teasing you. Don't worry about it. I'm going back there.

Ignatius   You're what?

Steffen   I'm gonna finish this and go back there and wait for him.

Ignatius   All night?

Steffen   Yeah. You wanna come?

Charlie *enters.*

Ignatius (*in English*)   He's going back to the flat to keep watching her to make sure –

Charlie (*in English*)   – she doesn't warn Brandt before we get there. Yeah. I thought he'd do that.

Charlie *and* **Steffen** *smile at one another.*

Steffen   Can I ask you something? What is the GDP of the Grosse Freiheit, do you think?

Ignatius   I have no idea.

Steffen   What about the Reeperbahn?

What about the cafés and the bars of St Georg?

Ignatius   Well not really a great deal I should imagine.

Steffen   Four and a half thousand million euros a year.

Ignatius (*in English*)   Four and a half thousand million euros is spent on prostitution in this city every year.

Charlie (*in English*)   Pricey.

Steffen   But that's just the money going to the girls. What about the money going to their taxi drivers? Or their hairdressers? Or the launderettes? And you think about what else their punters spend their money on and what happens to that money once they've spent it, don't you? When they've 'done their do', the punters go to the bars and spend the rest of their money. The bar owners take the punters' money and spend it on football matches. The football players spend their money on restaurants and the restaurateurs spend their money on the theatre and the brand new fucking Philharmonic Concert Hall. The money doesn't trickle down here. It trickles up. This whole city is built on the back of a Bulgarian teenager.

Ignatius (*in English*)   He's positing a specious economic argument.

Charlie (*in English*)   Terrific.

Steffen   Well. That's me.

What are you going to do now?

Ignatius   I'm going to go to bed.

Steffen   Good idea.

Ignatius   I've not been sleeping.

Steffen   No. You should drink a beer from the mini-bar maybe?

Ignatius   I think I've had enough.

Steffen   Yeah. Maybe you should have a bit of a wank watching the adverts for the sex-chat lines. That might help. They don't have those adverts in the UK, do they?

Ignatius   No, they don't.

Steffen   Maybe you should use a pillow. Fold it in two and fuck it. It's just an idea. Close your eyes and think of Julia Breitner.

Ignatius *is taken aback.*

Steffen   The records of exclusion at the Botany Department of Heidelberg University are remarkably well kept. Fourteen years old, Detective Stone. She must have been fabulous. I just thought I'd find out one or two things about you. Don't worry. I won't tell him anything.

He grins at **Ignatius**.

Steffen   Maybe you should just go and look for Kristina. She liked you, I think. You don't need to tell your dad about it. Go down to Brenner Reihe and get a room in the Stunde Hotel. I'll see you over there. I promise not to nick you.

Ignatius *decides not to translate this bit.*

Steffen   Right. You go to bed. I'll go to work. Tomorrow morning, Sergeant Stone. We'll get the fucker. I fucking promise you that. Good night.

Ignatius   Good night.

Steffen (*in English*)   Good night.

Charlie   Good night.

Steffen *leaves. Some time.* **Charlie** *and* **Ignatius** *speak in English.*

Charlie   Nice chap.

Ignatius   Lovely.

Charlie   Very inclusive. I completely trust him.

Ignatius   Yeah.

Charlie   'I'm sorry I don't speak any Germany' – it's 'I'm sorry I don't speak any German' not 'I'm sorry I don't speak any Germany'. Isn't it?

Ignatius   Yes, it is.

Charlie   You should have said. I feel like a bit of a cock now.

Ignatius   Sorry.

Charlie   I'm gonna get some sleep.

Ignatius   Lucky you.

Charlie   How long has it been now?

Ignatius   Five nights.

Charlie *looks at him.*

Nine

Stephanie*'s room, the hotel.* **Ignatius** *and* **Stephanie**.

Ignatius   I don't want to go to bed.

Stephanie   Why not?

Ignatius   I'm scared of going to sleep. What a weird thing to say. I'm sorry. I'll go.

Stephanie   You don't need to. It's good to see you. Nightmares are horrible.

Ignatius   Yeah. Yes. Yeah they are.

Stephanie   What were your nightmares about?

Ignatius   Before I came away I saw something on a DVD and I can't stop thinking about it. When I go to sleep it kind of plays out in my head.

Stephanie   That sounds awful.

Ignatius   Yeah.

Stephanie   Do you want a drink?

Ignatius   No. I drink too much. I drink all the time.

Stephanie   How are the seagulls?

Ignatius   Still awake.

Stephanie   You should shoot them or something.

Ignatius   I have thought about it.

Stephanie   It'd be funny, that. Watching you shoot a seagull from your hotel window. I'd love that.

Ignatius   Do you live here? In this hotel?

Stephanie   No.

Ignatius   What are you doing here, then?

Stephanie   I'm so sorry.

Ignatius   What about?

Stephanie   It doesn't matter.

Pause.

Ignatius   I love my wife very much.

Stephanie   I know that.

Ignatius   Do you ever get that feeling where it's like you're having rapid-eye movement when you're awake?

Stephanie   Here.

Ignatius   What?

Stephanie   Put your hand here. Can you feel that?

Ignatius   I think so.

Stephanie   When I touch you I feel so happy inside. Do you know what that is?

Ignatius   It feels like a bird. Or an animal or something. It's hard.

Stephanie   It's not an animal. Here. Look. You've got one too.

Ignatius   Yes. You even smell like her.

Stephanie   I know.

Ignatius   –

Stephanie   He's come back. He left for a while. He left Germany. He had to go to England on a business trip. He's back now. He's on the outside of the door. He's testing the door. You can see his shadow around the edges of the door if you think you're brave enough to look. He's trying to find a way in.

Ten

An interview room at the Police Stationon Steindamme. **Charlie**, **Steffen** *and* **Klaus Brandt**, *aka Klaus Brandt.*

Charlie (*in English*)   You would not believe the things we did to find you.

Ignatius   You would not believe the things we did to find you.

Charlie (*in English*)   We trawled the River Thames for two hours.

Ignatius   We trawled the River Thames for two hours.

Charlie (*in English*)   We watched hundreds and hundreds of hours of CCTV.

Ignatius   We watched hundreds and hundreds of hours of CCTV.

Klaus   I'm not saying anything until my lawyer gets here.

Ignatius   He's not saying anything until his laywer gets here.

Charlie (*in English*)   We interviewed over two hundred people in London.

Ignatius   We interviewed over two hundred people in London

Charlie (*in English*)   And now, Klaus Brandt, we've found you. Magic really, isn't it?

Klaus   I'm not saying anything until my lawyer gets here.

Ignatius (*in English*)   He really is quite insistent on some form of legal representative.

Charlie (*in English*)   Cute. Do the honours, Detective Stone.

Ignatius   Klaus Brandt, aka Klaus Brandt, I am arresting you for the murder of Vera Petrova, aka Vera Chislova, aka Vera Kukk, on the twentieth of May this year. You do not have to say anything, but it may harm your defence if you do not mention when questioned something that you later rely on in court. Anything you do say may be given in evidence. After your lawyer gets here we'll confirm your identity. We can take DNA samples to help us in the confirmation if you don't comply. We have a European Arrest Warrant for your apprehension. When your lawyer's here we will show that to you and explain to you exactly what it means. Basically you're coming back to England, where you should fully expect to be charged with and tried for the murder of Vera Petrova. You will be taken back on the next available flight. You will be accompanied by police from the KPD.

Do you understand what I just said to you?

Klaus   I'm not saying anything until my lawyer gets here.

Ignatius   I hope he's fucking great. (*In English.*) He's waiting to see his lawyer before he responds to anything. I told him I hoped he got a great one.

Steffen   Have you seen the video, by the way?

Klaus   I'm not saying anything until my lawyer gets here.

Steffen You've watched it, haven't you, Detective Stone? I knew you had.

Klaus I'm not saying anything until my lawyer gets here.

Charlie (*in English*)   Your semen was on her hair when her head was fished out of the river.

Ignatius Your semen was on her hair when her head was fished out of the river.

Charlie (*in English*)   You killed her by sticking her head in a vice and sawing it off at the neck with a hacksaw but before you did that you filmed yourself wanking in her hair and we found the traces of your semen.

Ignatius You killed her by sticking her head in a vice and sawing it off at the neck with a hacksaw but before you did that you filmed yourself wanking in her hair and found the traces of your semen.

Charlie (*in English*)   Was that Andres Rebane's idea?

Ignatius Was that Andres Rebane's idea?

Charlie (*in English*)   Did Andres Rebane force you to do that? So that your DNA would be left as evidence and the police would find you more easily?

Ignatius Did Andres Rebane force you to do that? So that your DNA would be left as evidence and the police would find you more easily.

Steffen *giggles.*

Charlie (*in English*)   When did you first meet Andres Rebane, Mr Becker?

Ignatius When did you first meet Andres Rebane?

Klaus *looks at them for a beat. Looks away.*

Ignatius How exactly do you know him?

Klaus *keeps looking away.*

Ignatius You did this for him, didn't you, Klaus? You didn't want to do it at all, did you?

Klaus I'm not saying anything until my lawyer gets here.

Charlie Where is he, Klaus? Where's Andres Rebane?

Ignatius He's the one we should really be talking to, isn't he, not you at all. You're just a cowardly lackey with a handsaw.

Klaus I'm not saying anything until my lawyer gets here.

Ignatius Is Andres Rebane also known as the White Bird?

Charlie (*in English*) I think it's quite important that you know that if you tell us where he is then that might militate in your favour when it comes to sentencing.

Ignatius Where is he?

Steffen *giggles a little.*

Charlie Where is he, Klaus?

Ignatius Who's the White Bird, Klaus?

Charlie (*in English*) Where is he, Klaus? Where's Andres Rebane?

Ignatius Where is he, Klaus? Where's Rebane?

Eleven

Steffen's *office. Later.* **Steffen**, **Charlie** *and* **Ignatius**.

Steffen We've contacted a colleague in Vice in Estonia. He knows Rebane. He says they'll find him within a week. They'll arrest him there. The speed Interpol move they'll be holding him there for years and years and years.

Ignatius Yeah. (*In English.*) They've contacted Vice in Estonia. They predict they'll get him within a week. Then it's up to Interpol.

Charlie (*in English*) Terrific.

Steffen If he's got any wits about him he'll sneak over to Narva. Cross the Russian border. Stroll into Kingisepp. Rob

a shop. Get nicked there. The Russians'll hold him for that.
They won't hand him over to be charged for the murder.
Certainly not to the Estonians.

Charlie (*in English*)   What did he say?

Ignatius (*in English*)   He's sceptical about the speed with
which we'll get our hands on him.

Charlie (*in English*)   Yeah.

Steffen   He's found Petrova's father. He's living outside
Tallinn.

Ignatius (*in English*)   They found Vera's father, outside
Tallinn.

Steffen   We'll keep you in touch.

Ignatius   Yes. Thank you.

Steffen   Or we could go.

Beat.

Ignatius   What?

Charlie (*in English*)   What did he just say?

Steffen   We could fucking drive there if you're afraid of
flying. Send Inspector Lee home with Brandt. Tell him we're
going to Tallinn to get a Victim Impact Statement from
Petrova's father. We could even go and do that. And then we
go into the apartments in Lasnamae and flush the bastard out.
Beat the fucking shit out of him. Lock him up in our hotel
room. Spend the night in the lap-dancing bars with the
EasyJet stag-weekenders. Drink a bottle of vodka. Find you
another fourteen-year-old girl. How much would you enjoy
that? That'd help you sleep a bit more easily, wouldn't it? Get
up the next day. Buffet breakfast in the hotel. Drive him back
here. Arrest him here. Nobody need ever know he was ever
there.

Ignatius   Are you joking?

Charlie (*in English*)   What did he ask you?

Ignatius   We couldn't do that. It would contravene every law of movement and arrest in international territory.

Charlie (*in English*)   What did you just say to him, Iggy?

Ignatius   It would expose us to so many charges of corruption and breaching police laws they could hang us by our toenails until our heads fell off.

Steffen   Yes. They could.

Charlie   Detective Stone, what did he just ask you?

Ignatius   It would be careless and stupid and reckless and endanger our investigation and help nobody.

Steffen   If you don't come with me you know what I'll do.

Charlie (*in English*)   What did he say? What did he say, Iggy? Iggy, what did he say to you?

Kultuur
kutsub
2011
TALLINN
NO99
teater | www.no99.
THREE
KINGDOMS
STEPHENS
NÜBLING
SEMPER
Esietendus 17. september 2011
Koos teatritega Münchner Kammerspiele ja Lyric Hammersmith

Part Three: Tallinn

Rudi *Do you want me to tell you the truth about
this country?*
Ignatius *The truth?*

Rudi *Soll ich dir mal die Wahrheit über unser
Land erzählen?*
Ignatius *Die Wahrheit?*

Rudi *Tahad, ma räägin sulle tõtt selle riigi kohta?*
Ignatius *Tõtt?*

One

A room in an apartment in the Lasnamae, Tallinn. **Tom, Michael, Fredo** *and* **Sonny** *are not the real names of the men here.* **Tom** *is* **Andres Rebane. Fredo** *is* **Rudi Peiker. Michael** *is* **Mart Oper. Sonny** *is* **Kristen Reims. Olya** *is with them. She is their prisoner.*

Michael   I think that's one of the things that our customers appreciate about what we do.

Sonny   We're not like some fucking Romanian product.

Michael   In comparison to the product coming out of certain areas of Warsaw, for example.

Sonny   Polish-junky fuck-houses.

Michael   And the communication lines are good.

Sonny   North African nigger pussy.

Michael   That was the most striking lesson from my last trip, I think.

Tom   Michael, with respect. Your last trip was two years ago.

Sonny   Little bits of Chinese rubber chicken.

Michael   Sonny.

Sonny   Sorry, Michael.

Tom   Nobody's expanding, Michael.

Michael   They should be.

Tom   You go over to London. You go over to Frankfurt. You go over to Paris. Everybody's holding their hands very close to their chests.

Michael   They're making a mistake.

Sonny   'Cause they're fucking stupid cunt-holes.

Tom   If we expanded now and we found that the demand for our product was finite –

Michael   It's not.

Tom   We don't know that, Michael.

Michael   We do. The real advantage in our market is that demand is always, has always been and will always be stable.

We have the potential now to establish an acute niche identity. It's practically boutique.

Tom   I'm just not sure that it's strong enough to justify the kind of investment that the kind of expansion you're talking about will entail.

Michael   People are exhausted by the tedium of globalisation. They're searching for an affirmation of identity through the possibility that their experience, established by what they consume, is particular and unique. There is a hunger for authenticity. We can provide that.

Tom   Michael, you know how much I respect you.

Michael *looks at him, says nothing.*

Tom   You know I'm not trying to undermine you.

Michael *looks at him, says nothing.*

Sonny   Is she any better?

Fredo   Not bad. She's a bit – I was going to use the word 'inert'.

Tom   Has she fallen asleep?

Fredo   I didn't notice.

Sonny   She's fucking quiet. She never says a fucking word. Dumb cunt.

Fredo   I'm not entirely sure she can actually speak Estonian

Sonny   I don't think she can fucking speak anything.

She just sits there like a fucking spastic mongoloid. Whimpering. Cunt.

We should give her a name.

Tom   She's got a name.

Sonny   No, a different name. Like a pet's name. Like a dog's name.

Fredo   Like Fido or something.

Sonny   Train her to fetch our slippers. Train her to make us a gin and tonic. Train her to do something useful instead of just sitting there all day sucking our cocks and fucking whimpering in a language I can't even fucking understand.

I love this feeling.

Fredo   Yes.

Sonny   I feel so alive.

Fredo   Yes.

Are you OK, Michael?

What's on your mind?

They look at him.

Michael   A man's character is moulded by two things.

They look at him.

By his everyday work, and the material resources which he thereby procures.

They look at him.

Michael   I don't believe profit-making is essentially evil.

Sonny   Me neither.

Tom   Don't you?

Michael   No, I really don't.

Tom   You should see some of the things that I've seen.

Sonny   With the fucking cock-sucking pigeon-shits.

Michael   You know what are the four virtues of doing business? There is Prudence – to buy low and sell high. There is Temperance – to save and accumulate. There is Justice –

to pay willingly for good work. And there is Courage – the courage to venture on new ways of business. To overcome the fear of change, to bear defeat unto bankruptcy, to be courteous to new ideas, to wake up next morning and face fresh work with cheer. And there is Love. The love involved in the process of taking care of one's own. Love involved in taking care of employees and partners and colleagues and customers and fellow citizens, to wish well of humankind, to seek God, finding humanity in the marketplace.

In the future we'll be finding girls in London and selling them to Beijing. We'll be finding girls in Paris and selling them to Mumbai. We'll be finding girls in Frankfurt and selling them to Rio de Janeiro. We'll be finding girls in Amsterdam and selling them to Moscow.

Some time.

Fredo   Have we got any food?

Tom   I'm hungry, actually.

Sonny   We should get a fucking pizza or something.

Fredo   We could call out.

Tom   Or just go down to Vapiano.

Fredo   Oh, nice.

Michael   I like the pizzas at Vapiano. Their dough is so fresh. They cook it beautifully.

Fredo   Yes.

Sonny   I'll go down. I could do with a walk. I could do with stretching my legs. They're a bit weak.

Michael   I'll come with you.

Sonny   Stay with Fido, yes? Give her a bone or something.

Tom   Do you need some money?

Sonny   Fuck you, Tom. No, I don't need some fucking money.

Tom   I was only offering.

Sonny   Do I look like I can't afford to buy pizza?

Tom   It was just an offer.

Sonny   Yeah, well, fuck you.

Tom   I'll have a Four Seasons.

Sonny   'Do you need some money?'

Fredo   I'll have an Americano Hot.

Michael   Kick her if she moves.

Sonny   'Do you need some fucking money?' Cunt.

He leaves with **Michael**. *There is some time.*

Tom   She's ugly this one, eh?

Fredo   And she stinks now.

Tom   It's been two days.

Fredo   Even so. A bit of fucking perfume wouldn't hurt, would it?

Tom   I think she's mentally handicapped, by the way. I'm completely serious. Have you heard her trying to speak? She doesn't know fucking anything. She doesn't even know who our fucking prime minister is. What's the name of our prime minister? Hey. Hey. Hey, Fido. Hey, Fido.

Olya   My name isn't Fido.

Tom   Fuck you, bitch. Fido. What is the name of our fucking prime minister?

Olya   Please God, stop.

Fredo   God. Did she just say God?

Tom   Did you just say God, Fido, you thick bit of cunt. Fido, did nobody tell you, Fido, that this is a secular state?

Olya   My name isn't Fido.

Tom (*to* **Olya**)   Funny. You look exactly like her.

Fredo   What are you doing tonight?

Tom   Tonight? Nothing, why?

Fredo   You know the Radisson Blu?

Tom   What about it?

Fredo   I'll text you my room number. Meet me there. About nine o'clock.

Tom   Why?

Fredo   Why do you think?

Tom   I have no idea.

Is this to do with . . . ?

Have you been working behind Sonny's back?

Have you been dealing directly with the White Bird?

Right. Wow. Fuck.

Fuck.

Two

The house of Vera Petrova's father. **Mr Petrov**, **Steffen Dresner**, *the* **Translator** (*the same* **Translator** *as was used in London, but dressed as* **Mart Oper**), *DS* **Ignatius Stone**.

Ignatius (*in English*)   Mr Petrov, I understand how hard this must be for you.

Translator (*in Estonian*)   Mr Petrov, I understand how hard this must be for you.

Mr Petrov *looks at them blankly. Looks away.*

Ignatius (*in English*)   Maybe you could tell us a little about what she was like as a child. Or you could talk perhaps about the emotional impact of this crime on your life.

Translator (*in Estonian*)   Maybe you could tell us a little about what she was like as a child. Or you could talk perhaps about the emotional impact of this crime on your life.

Ignatius (*in English*)   This kind of detail could add several years to the sentencing of the man who did this to your daughter.

Translator (*in Estonian*)   This kind of detail could add several years to the sentencing of the man who did this to your daughter.

Mr Petrov *looks at them blankly. Looks away.*

Mr Petrov (*in Estonian*)   She was a whore. She was a pain in the arse. She lied. All the time. She had no friends. She smelt fucking disgusting. I really, you know, hated her. I'm not sad. She deserved it. It was always going to happen one day. It was just a question of time.

Translator (*in English*)   She was a whore. She was a pain in the arse. She lied. All the time. She had no friends. She smelt fucking disgusting. I really, you know, hated her. I'm not sad. She deserved it. It was always going to happen one day. It was just a question of time.

Ignatius *stares at him.*

Three

A hotel room in the Radisson Blu, Tallinn. **Rudi Peiker** *waits for* **Andres Rebane** *with* **Steffen Dresner** *and DS* **Ignatius Stone**. **Steffen Dresner** *speaks in German unless stated otherwise.* **Ignatius Stone** *speaks in English unless stated otherwise.* **Peiker** *alternates between German and English and Estonian. As* **Peiker** *talks he completely changes his clothes. He maybe drinks some shots of vodka which he shares with* **Dresner** *and* **Stone**. *He maybe takes some cocaine which he shares with them too.* **Ignatius** *might refuse it.*

Rudi   How was your journey?

Steffen   Fine.

Rudi   The ferries?

Steffen   They were calm. It was all good.

Rudi   How long did it take you?

Steffen   About nineteen hours.

Rudi   Yeah. Figures. Andres did it in seventeen. But he's a fucking maniac.

Ignatius   This is the furthest north I've ever been.

Rudi (*in English*)   Yeah?

Ignatius   Yeah. And the furthest east.

Rudi (*in English*)   Nice.

Steffen   Fucking English, eh?

Rudi (*in English*)   How do you find it?

Ignatius   What?

Rudi (*in English*)   Estonia?

Ignatius   I've hardly seen it. I've only been here a couple of hours.

Rudi (*in English*)   But basing it on what you've seen.

Ignatius   It's very clean.

Rudi   It is.

Ignatius   It's very bright. For nine o'clock.

Rudi (*in English*)   It won't get dark tonight.

Ignatius   What?

Rudi (*in English*)   Maybe at one in the morning. For a bit.

Ignatius   Shit.

Rudi   Yeah. It frightens some people. They find it difficult to sleep.

Steffen   We won't worry about that, I think.

Ignatius   This hotel's nice.

Rudi   Yes.

Ignatius   There's a remarkable system for charging things from the mini-bar. It's like the mini-bar electronically registers when you've taken something out of the fridge. And charges it straight to your room account. That was quite impressive to me.

Steffen *and* **Rudi** *examine him for a bemused beat.*

Rudi (*in English*)   We're a very technological country. It's like a fucking – what? A fucking religion. Not what you thought we would be, I bet?

Ignatius   I had no idea what to think.

Rudi   No. But I know what fucking English people think about us. I've seen their football commentaries. I don't think they know the difference between the Baltic Sea and the Balkan Sea half the time. Yes? Am I right? You know how much confidence there is in us lot here?

Ignatius   I don't really know what you're talking about.

Rudi   Ninety-two per cent of people when asked if they had confidence in the Estonian police answered that yes, they did. How high would that figure be in London?

Ignatius   I've no idea.

Rudi   No. How the fuck are you, Steffen?

Steffen   I'm fucking tired.

Rudi   Yeah.

Steffen   I need a fucking drink.

Rudi   Good.

Steffen   I need to get out. Go and see the town. Have a bit of a fucking rest and recuperation, you with me?

Rudi   How was Mr Petrov?

Steffen   I really liked him. He was fucking funny, Iggy, wasn't he?

Ignatius *doesn't answer.*

Steffen   He really cheered us both up.

Rudi   Great. Well. We'll finish this. Then maybe we've got a bit of free time to enjoy ourselves.

Ignatius   Is he coming here?

Rudi   Who?

Ignatius   Rebane?

Rudi   He'll be here in about ten minutes.

Ignatius   Right.

Steffen   Good. Great. Fuck. Get this thing fucking over and done with, yeah? Can we keep him here?

Rudi   Oh fuck yes.

Ignatius   How do you know him?

Rudi   I've been working with him undercover for three years.

Ignatius   What's he like?

Rudi (*in English*)   Young. Stupid. Ugly. Estonian.

Ignatius   Estonian?

Rudi (*in English*)   Everybody assumes the people involved in this line of work here are Russian immigrants. They're not. The girls are. The boys who sell them are middle-class Estonian boys born and bred.

He receives a text. Sends a reply.

Between December and March this lot and a group in Kopli moved ten girls into the West. That's fucking nothing, eh?

In a population of a million and a quarter. That's the equivalent of two hundred Romanians in three months. Or eight Germans.

He's a fuck-hole. Just get him out to Hamburg as soon as you can and arrest him there and leave me to get on with the rest of them here. They like to pretend they're gangsters. They're not. They give each other nicknames from the fucking *Godfather* for godsake. Sonny. Michael. Rebane calls himself Tom. After Tom Hagan. The adopted son.

Steffen   Robert Duvall.

Rudi   Precisely.

Steffen   Who's Fredo?

Rudi   Me.

Steffen   Nice.

Ignatius   Is one of them ever known as the White Bird?

Rudi *and* **Steffen** *look at him. Some time.*

Rudi   Where did you hear about the White Bird?

Steffen *smiles. Hums the tune.*

Ignatius   Aleksandr Richter talked about him when we arrested him. Have you heard his name before?

Rudi   A few times. What have you heard about him?

Ignatius   Not a great deal. Richter described him as an evil fuck. Nobody else in London or Hamburg seems to have the slightest idea who he is.

Rudi   No?

Steffen   Funny, that.

Ignatius   What do you know about him?

Rudi   His name's been mentioned in connection to some of the work that Rebane's been involved with. There's rumour that he's in some way significant. There's a bar in the centre of the town, at the back of the old cathedral, where people claim he drinks in. The Dragon. It's a hole of a place. We've had it under surveillance before. We've never found anything.

Ignatius   If I wanted to find him is that where I should look?

Rudi   Yeah. I think it is. Do you want to find him?

Ignatius   Yes. I think I do.

Rudi   Are you fucking sure?

Ignatius   Yes. I think I am.

Rudi *smiles.*

Rudi   Good for you.

He receives a text. Checks it.

Right. That's Rebane. He's here. He's on his way up.

Ignatius (*in English*)   He's here?

Rudi (*in English*)   In the lobby. He just arrived. I sent him the room number. (*In German.*) So. We know what we're doing, yes?

Steffen   I think so.

Ignatius   I don't.

Rudi   Well. Just watch. Stay out of the way. It won't last long.

Ignatius   What won't last too long?

Steffen   'What won't last too long?' Fuck. What do you fucking think?

Ignatius   I have no idea.

Steffen   'I have no idea.' Have you heard the way he fucking talks? Fuck.

Rudi   I like this bit.

Steffen   Yeah?

Rudi   Getting into character.

Steffen   Yeah.

Rudi   Lights. Camera. Action.

The buzzer at the door goes.

Steffen   Ha.

Rudi   OK.

They open the door. They let in **Andres Rebane**.

Andres (*in Estonian*)   Hey.

Rudi (*in Estonian*)   Hey, Tom.

Andres (*in Estonian*)   Nice fucking place no?

Rudi (*in Estonian*)   Yeah. It's good. It's sweet. Come in.

Andres (*in Estonian*)   I like the sign for the fucking disco.
Good Disco All The Time. That's sounds fucking cool, man.
We should come.

Rudi (*in Estonian*)   Yeah.

Andres (*in German now*)   Hey, man.

Steffen   What?

Andres   How are you, man?

Steffen   I'm OK.

Andres   What's up?

Steffen   What are you talking about?

Andres   I've not seen you for months, man, who's your
friend?

Steffen   I think you've made something of a mistake.

Andres   What?

Steffen   I have no idea where you think we've met one
another before but really we haven't.

Andres   What? In fucking, in . . . in . . .

Steffen   Were you confusing me for somebody else?

Andres   –

Steffen   Were you confusing me for somebody else maybe?
That happens.

Rudi *has moved behind* **Andres**. *Grabs him in a stranglehold with a belt.* **Dresner** *hits him five times in the belly. He breaks ribs.* **Rebane** *cries.*

Steffen   Stop fucking crying, killer. You're meant to be fucking Tom Hagan for fucksake. Does Tom Hagan fucking cry? Does Robert Duvall fucking cry you fucking pussy?

Ignatius (*in English*)   Fuck.

Rudi *takes some handcuffs from his inside pocket and straps them on* **Andres**.

Andres (*in Estonian*)   Oh fuck. Oh fuck. Oh fuck. Are you fucking police, Fredo? Fredo, are you fucking police, man?

Dresner *hits him three more times.*

Ignatius (*in English*)   Fuck.

Steffen   What?

Ignatius   Nothing.

Steffen   What?

Ignatius   Nothing really.

Steffen   No, what, Iggy? Fucking what, man? Here.

Ignatius   What?

Steffen   Your turn.

Ignatius   Fuck off.

Steffen   Iggy. Seriously.

Ignatius   I'd rather not Steffen, thank you, no, I'd rather –

Steffen   Don't, Iggy. I've been driving you here all day, man, I'm exhausted. Don't let me down now. Hit him.

Ignatius *looks at him.*

Steffen   It will feel fucking amazing. You're a cop, for fuck's sake, you can do whatever you want. You know what he's done. You've seen the fucking DVD.

Ignatius *hits* **Andres**. *He hits him again.*

Steffen   That's better.

And then **Ignatius** *hits him again twice, harder, getting really into it.*

Rudi   I love this feeling.

Steffen   Fuck, yes.

Rudi   We should go to The Dragon.

Steffen   Are you serious?

Rudi   Go drinking. Call some girls. Celebrate. I bet he's fucking here.

Ignatius   You bet who's here?

Rudi   Who do you think?

Ignatius   The White Bird? What do you mean, 'he's here'?

Rudi   He's here. In Tallinn. Now. Right now. He's here. I know he is. I'm feeling fucking lucky. I can feel it in my bones.

Four

The Dragon. A basement bar, deep under the ground, in the heart of Tallinn. **Rudi Peiker,** *DS* **Ignatius Stone** *and* **Steffen Dresner** *are drinking.* **Rudi** *pours shot after shot of vodka down his throat and expects* **Steffen** *and* **Ignatius** *to do the same.* **Ignatius** *and* **Steffen** *and* **Rudi** *are also eating a big bowl of cowslips.*

With them are two women. One, **Liisi,** *looks exactly like* **Stephanie Friedmann**. *Her face is very badly battered. The other,* **Liisu,** *looks exactly like* **Hele Kachonov**.

The women drink.

Mr Petrov *sits alone talking into his vodka.*

Nobody else seems to notice that he is there.

Rudi *(in English)*   Have you met my wife?

Ignatius   No. No. I haven't. No. What time is it?

Rudi   This is my wife. Liisi.

Ignatius   Hello. What time is it, Rudi? What time is he arriving?

Rudi   This is her best friend. Liisu. Liisi, Liisu, say hello to Detective Ignatius Stone.

Liisi   Hello.

Liisu   Hello.

Ignatius   Hi. Hello. Hello.

Rudi   Have another shot.

Ignatius   Thank you.

Rudi   It's good, no?

Ignatius   It's very sweet.

Rudi   Isn't it?

Mr Petrov   It was the Nazis who brought the whisky here.

Ignatius   We're the only ones here, Rudi.

Rudi   I noticed that.

Ignatius   Is it worth waiting for him or should we just go?

Rudi   If you want to. Calm down.

Ignatius   I am calm.

Rudi   You're being fucking restless. It's getting on my nerves, man.

Ignatius   I've been searching for him for a long time.

Rudi   And you've nearly found him. So relax. Eat.

Mr Petrov   They fucking loved this place. There were swastikas on all the panels. You can imagine them, no? Everybody here thought they were so fucking cool, you know? With their Hugo Boss uniforms. And their dancing. And their little packets of German sweeties.

They drink.

Fuck I used to love those sweeties.

They drink.

Ignatius   What are these?

Rudi   They're cowslips.

Ignatius   Cowslips?

Rudi   Cowslip *Primula veris*. In sugar.

Ignatius   What are you meant to do with them?

Rudi   You're meant to eat them.

Ignatius   Eat them?

Rudi   Yeah.

Ignatius   Flowers?

Rudi   That's right.

Ignatius *eats them. Tentatively. The others watch him.*

Rudi   How are they?

Ignatius   They're –

Steffen   Fucking lovely. no?

He takes a handful and eats it whole. They all laugh at him.

He was funny in the hotel room, wasn't he?

He bursts out laughing too.

I thought you were going to piss your fucking pants. Here.

They drink.

Mr Petrov   Knowledge is overrated.

They drink.

Knowledge has been replaced by money. It's simpler. It's beautiful.

Ignatius *turns to* **Liisi**.

Ignatius (*in English*)   I think this vodka's stronger than I'm used to. (*To* **Liisi**.) What happened to your face?

Liisi (*in Estonian*)   What?

Ignatius (*in English*)   I'm sorry. You look like somebody I know. I don't think you are her.

She kisses **Rudi**. *He kisses her back.*

Liisi (*in Estonian*)   Your friend's pretty fucking strange, Rudi, eh?

Ignatius (*in English*)   Are you two married?

Rudi   Don't be so impatient, Detective Stone. It's a characteristic of your nationality.

They drink.

Mr Petrov   Everything will fall apart. In the future regions will hold referendums and vote for independence. And then towns will hold referendums and vote for independence. And then neighbourhoods. And then whole streets. And then families and then individuals. Children will have referendums voting for independence from their parents.

The whole fucking ship is going down.

They drink.

Rudi   Do you want me to tell you the truth about this country?

Ignatius   The truth?

The women look at him. Smile at each other. Drink some more. **Steffen** *and* **Rudi** *drink some more.* **Liisi** *keeps kissing* **Rudi** *as he talks, as though trying to distract him from what he's trying to say.*

Rudi (*in German*)   The plague fucked us. The famine fucked us. The Swedes fucked us. The Germans fucked us. The Russians fucked us. But most of all. At the heart of it, was you. It was you, Ignatius. Nobody else. It was all you. (*In English.*) You fucked us. Cheers.

They drink.

Liisi, **Liisu** *and* **Steffen**   Cheers.

Ignatius   I don't care. I don't give a shit. I don't give a shit. I don't give a shit. I don't give a shit. I don't give a shit about what happens to your fucking country. I honestly don't care. Look into my fucking eyes and ask me if you think I really care. I just think your women are quite sexy. I just think your vodka is surprisingly sweet. And that finally your clothes are a bit more shit than mine.

Liisu (*in Estonian*)   You should take him into the woods. That'd relax him.

Rudi   She thinks I should take you into the woods.

Liisu (*in Estonian*)   The woods here are full of demons.

Rudi   She said the woods here are full of demons.

Liisi   Don't you think that she looks like someone you know?

Liisu (*in Estonian*)   Did you like my friend's DVD?

Ignatius   I'm sorry, I really can't understand what you're saying.

Liisi   She asked you if you liked my DVD?

Ignatius   What DVD?

Liisu (*in Estonian*)   When you watched it you got a hard on.

Liisi   She says she knows what happened to you when you watched it.

Liisu (*in Estonian*)   Is there something you need to ask us?

Liisi   She wants to know if there's something you need to ask us.

Liisu (*in Estonian*)   Have you figured out what the White Bird is yet?

Liisi   She wants to know if you've figured out what the White Bird is yet?

Ignatius   What do you mean? What does that mean, 'if I've figured out what the White Bird is'? What do you know about the White Bird?

Liisu (*in Estonian*)   When you close your eyes do you see yourself in that room?

Liisi   When you close your eyes do you see yourself in that room?

Liisu (*in Estonian*)   With that woman who looks exactly like your wife?

Liisi   With that woman who looks exactly like your wife?

Liisu (*in Estonian*)   Doing all those things to her that you saw on the DVD?

Liisi   Doing all of those things that you saw on the DVD.

She starts laughing at him.

Ignatius   Why did she say 'what' the White Bird is? Not 'who'?

Steffen   I'm sorry?

Ignatius   I don't understand why she asked me if I'd figured out 'what' the White Bird is, not 'who' he is.

Steffen   Is everything OK, Detective Stone?

Ignatius   Is he here?

Steffen   Is who here?

Ignatius   Have I been here before?

Steffen   Where?

Ignatius   In this hotel room.

Steffen   This isn't a hotel room.

Ignatius   How did you know where Rebane was?

Steffen   Rudi told me. You know that. You were there when he told me.

Ignatius   How do you know Rudi?

Steffen   How do you imagine I know Rudi?

Ignatius   He spoke German to you, Rebane, when he saw you. Why did he speak German to you? How did he know you were German? Who told Rebane that Vera Petrova was talking to the police?

Steffen   Somebody inside the police.

Ignatius   It was you.

Steffen   What?

Ignatius   It was you.

Steffen   What was me?

What was me, Iggy?

Ignatius   Oh. Oh. Oh. Oh. Fuck.

Steffen   You've got to admit it's quite funny.

Ignatius   Oh no. Oh fuck. Oh no.

Ignatius   Oh no.

Steffen   Cheer up, Ignatius. You got Rebane. You got Brandt. You got the bad guys. Great. Good work. Well done. You're a fucking hero.

After some of the things that you've done.

Ignatius   It was you, all this time.

Steffen   You didn't need to hurt her.

Ignatius   Hurt who?

Steffen   Stephanie Friedmann.

Ignatius   I didn't hurt her. I don't know what you're talking about.

Rudi   Ask him how old he is.

Ignatius   How old are you?

Steffen   How old do you think?

Rudi   Ask him again.

Ignatius   How old are you?

Steffen   Hundreds and hundreds and hundreds and hundreds of years old.

Ignatius   What?

Steffen   Be sober, be vigilant; because your adversary as a roaring lion walketh about seeking whom he may devour.

Don't panic. I can't get inside your head.

Well, I can.

Ignatius   What?

Steffen   I can get inside your head. I'm kind of, I'm kind of there now.

Iggy. Do you know how old she is? Liisu, Iggy? She's fourteen.

Ignatius   The man outside the William Morris. It was you.

Steffen   Did you honestly think you could stop me?

Ignatius   When Aleksandr Richter said he was an 'evil fuck' he was talking about you.

Steffen   I'm not evil, Iggy. I only sell things that people want to buy. Ask her if she wants to go with you to your room.

Ignatius   No.

Steffen   Ask her.

Ignatius   Do you want to go with me to my room?

Liisu   Yes.

Ignatius   Did your face just change?

Steffen   My what?

Ignatius   Just now. When I looked away. *Your face. Did it just change?*

Steffen   My face?

Ignatius   I thought your face changed.

Steffen   What do you mean? Did I pull a funny face?

Ignatius   No. It became a different person's face. Your eyes changed colour. Suddenly you were old.

Steffen   Can I give you a word of advice?

It's really, really serious.

You must never say a word about me to anyone you ever meet ever in your whole life again.

From this moment on, for the rest of your life, don't ever shut your eyes.

Ignatius   What?

Steffen   From this moment on when you see the images that are playing on the inside of your head, then the inside of your head will burst into flames.

Five

The next morning **Ignatius Stone** *goes to check out of his hotel. The* **Receptionist** *looks exactly like* **Tommy White**. *He speaks in very bad Estonian with a very strong English accent. There is thick red blood all down* **Ignatius**'*s shirt.* **Ignatius** *speaks in English.*

Ignatius   Where's Dresner?

Receptionist   –

Ignatius   Where's Dresner?

Receptionist   –

Ignatius   Where's he gone?

Receptionist   I'm sorry, sir?

Ignatius   Steffen Dresner?

Receptionist   I don't really know who you're talking about.

Ignatius   I'm looking for a guest who is staying in this hotel. My colleague. Steffen Dresner. D-R-E-S-N-E-R.

Tommy? Tommy? What are you doing here?

Receptionist   I don't really know who you're talking about.

Ignatius   What the fuck are you doing here, Tommy?

Receptionist   I don't really know who you're talking about.

Six

An office in a central Tallinn police station. **Ignatius Stone** *is being interrogated by two members of the Tallinn Police Force. They look very much like* **Sonny** *and* **Michael**. **Michael** *speaks in English.*

Ignatius   Why are you looking at me like that?

Sonny   Don't you remember?

Michael   Don't you remember?

Ignatius   What?

Sonny   What you did? What you said? Have you forgotten what you did?

Michael   What you did? What you said? Have you forgotten what you did?

Ignatius   –

Sonny   Seriously, Detective Stone. Have you forgotten?

Michael   Seriously, Detective Stone. Have you forgotten?

Ignatius   What have I done?

Sonny   We found Stephanie Friedmann in your bathroom. She'd been bleeding for some time. She's in hospital. She told us that she wouldn't press charges. But fucking hell, Detective Stone.

Michael   It's all right. Nobody knows you're here. We can cover this over. I've spoken to the head of the crime squad. He understands about the pressure of these things. But really, after what you did to Vera Petrova.

Ignatius   I don't know what you're talking about.

You're starting to scare me.

Sonny   Yeah.

He leaves.

Ignatius   You're not seriously suggesting – You're not seriously . . . You're not seriously suggesting . . .

Michael   You fell asleep.

Ignatius   Did I?

Michael   As soon as we brought you in here.

Ignatius   I've been – I'm quite tired.

Michael   You know what guilty people do when they're left alone in an interview room, don't you, Detective Stone? They sleep for hours and hours and hours.

Sonny *re-enters. He has a hammer in a clear plastic evidence bag. He takes it out, holding it with a handkerchief. He puts it on the table.*

Sonny   Your prints are all over this.

Michael   Your prints are all over this.

Sonny   She'll survive. She'll recover. The hospital in Tartu is really extraordinary.

Michael   She'll survive. She'll recover. The hospital in Tartu is really extraordinary.

Sonny   Wipe it.

Michael   Wipe it.

Ignatius   What?

Sonny *and* **Michael** *look at him. He takes the handkerchief and wipes the hammer.*

Sonny   What's your full name?

Michael   What's your full name?

Ignatius   I, er –

Charlie   Can't you remember?

Ignatius   No. I'm really trying to. Are you police officers?

Sonny   Are we police officers? Is that what he just asked us?

Ignatius   Am I under arrest?

Sonny   He's funny.

Michael   He's like my favourite comedian ever.

Sonny   Are you English or American?

Michael   Are you English or American?

Ignatius   Am I English?

Michael   Yes. English. Do you come from England? Or America?

Ignatius   I think I am English.

Michael   I thought so too.

Sonny   Are you lying?

Michael   He wants to know if you're lying.

Ignatius   I don't know.

Sonny   I'm afraid your card's been turned down. At the hotel reception.

Charlie   Yeah. Funny that. We're afraid your card's been turned down. At the hotel reception.

Sonny   And we looked at your passport.

Michael   And we looked at your passport. It was very good. A really good bit of work. But not as good as if you'd got it

done here. Because really. The passport forgery done in Kopli
is just out of this world nowadays.

Ignatius   It wasn't a forgery.

Michael   No?

Ignatius   Of course it wasn't.

Sonny   Do you honestly expect us to believe that you're
name is Ignatius, Paul?

Michael   What kind of name is Ignatius, Paul, really?

Ignatius   I'm not called Paul.

Sonny   Here. What does it say here? Is that your photograph?
Is that your fucking photograph, you lying, drunken English
fucking cunt?

Michael   Is that your photograph in this passport?

Ignatius   Yes. It's my photograph.

Charlie   And what does that name say?

Ignatius   It says that my name is Paul Stone.

Michael   Paul. See. Like Paul McCartney.

Sonny   Maybe some coffee.

Michael   Would you like some coffee?

Ignatius   Yes. I would please.

Sonny   Here.

Ignatius   Thank you.

Michael   How does it taste?

Ignatius   Yes. Good yes. It's very hot. Have you put
something in it?

They smile at him.

He slumps in his chair. Slams his head on the table.

Michael *pours the coffee on his face. He wakes up screaming.*

Sonny   What do you think we should do with you?

Michael   What do you think we should do with you?

Sonny   Paul?

Michael   Paul?

Sonny   What do you think we should do with you?

Michael   What do you think we should do with you?

Ignatius   I don't know.

Michael   No. I know you don't know, but have a fucking think for Christ's sake, Paul, you stupid fucking cunt.

Ignatius   I want to go home.

Michael   Do you?

Ignatius   I want to see my wife.

Michael   Your what? (*In Estonian.*) He wants to see his wife.

Sonny   His fucking what?

Michael   Here.

Ignatius   What?

Sonny   Look over there.

Ignatius   What?

Ignatius *turns his head.* **Sonny** *smacks him hard.*

Sonny   What do you think we should do with you?

Michael   What do you think we should do with you?

Ignatius   You need to listen to me very carefully. Steffen Dresner is not who he says he is. He is a very dangerous man. He calls himself the White Bird.

Sonny   Do you think this is what we do?

Michael   Do you think this is how we behave?

Ignatius   You have to stop him. You have to leave here now and stop Steffen Dresner.

Sonny Do you know the slightest fucking thing about our country, Paul, you fucking little tourist?

Wait here. I'm going to get the shotgun.

Ignatius What?

Sonny Blow his fucking brains out.

Here. On the table. There's chocolate. There's vodka. There's a small glass of liquid cyanide. Drink the cyanide. Drink the vodka. Eat the chocolate. If you've not done this by the time I come back in I will blow your brains against the fucking wall. Do you understand me?

Michael Here. On the table. There's chocolate. There's vodka. There's a small glass of liquid cyanide. Drink the cyanide. Drink the vodka. Eat the chocolate. If you've not done this by the time we come back in he will blow your brains against the fucking wall. Do you understand me?

Sonny Do you understand me?

Michael Do you understand him?

Sonny Do you understand me, Paul?

Michael Do you understand him, Paul?

Seven

They leave. **Ignatius** *looks at the cyanide. He looks at it for a long time. He picks it up. He holds it to his nose. He sniffs it. He cries. He drinks it. He drinks the vodka. He eats the chocolate. He waits.*

Detective Inspector **Martin Lemsalu** *enters. He is dressed immaculately. DI* **Charlie Lee** *is with him.*

Martin Detective Stone? My name is Detective Inspector Martin Lemsalu of the Tallinn Crime Department.

Ignatius Charlie?

Charlie Ignatius.

Ignatius   What are you doing here?

Charlie   What do you think?

Martin   We've checked you in. Your flight leaves in just over an hour. We can drive you to the airport. It's amazingly close. It's practically round the corner. It's a small airport too, so there's no need to get there too early.

Ignatius   Have I been asleep while I've been waiting for you?

Lemsalu *doesn't quite know how to respond to this, so he ignores the question.*

Martin   We heard about your friend Dresner.

Ignatius   What did you hear about him?

Martin   Ha. That's a good one.

Charlie *smiles too.*

Martin   He went back.

Ignatius   To Hamburg?

Martin   Yes, of course to Hamburg. He was driven back this morning. He's a bit of a party animal, I think. Yes? He has an eye for the ladies, doesn't he?

Ignatius   It was him. He was involved in moving the girls into Hamburg. He told Rebane that the British police had tried to find him. He got Rebane to have Vera executed. He was the man in the William Morris with Tommy White. The German who giggled, Charlie, it was him. You can't let him go. Charlie, tell him. He's the White Bird. Dresner is the White Bird, Charlie I swear.

Charlie *can barely look at him.*

Martin *smiles as a means of avoiding this palpably embarrassing contention.*

Ignatius   How long have I been here?

Martin   What?

Ignatius   How long have I been waiting here? How did I get into this room?

Martin *smiles as a means of avoiding this palpably embarrassing question.*

Charlie   This is embarrassing.

He leaves.

Martin   Maybe you'd like some coffee before your car gets here.

He pours him a cup of coffee. **Ignatius** *sips it. It tastes lovely.*

Ignatius   Where's Andres Rebane?

Martin   He's been arrested.

Ignatius   That's –

Martin   In Pihkva. He robbed a jeweller's.

Ignatius   He what?

Martin   The Russian police won't release him. Pihkva is an ancient city in the north-west of Russia. He went over there on a speedboat or something very early this morning. Robbed a jeweller's. Got himself arrested. The Russian police won't release him until they've charged him for robbery. He'll be tried there.

Ignatius   They –

Martin   They won't agree to release him to face charges here. They're holding him for the robbery. It'll drag on. Until somebody pays enough money for him to be released. Which they will. It happens.

But we got his colleagues. Kristen Reims, twenty-seven. Mart Oper, twenty-nine. It was your leads with Rebane who led us to them. Which is one good thing, no? They're going to go to jail for a very fucking long time. You should see our State Prosecutor. He's a really good guy. He wears really nice jeans.

Ignatius   Jeans?

Martin   I really like his jeans. They're smart but they're kind of cool. He doesn't iron them or anything like that, you know.

Ignatius   She was my wife's age. Vera Petrova.

Martin   You know there is one gang. You can't define a country by one gang, Detective Stone, can you? There are four men. They have done very little damage. Compared to what happens in London. Compared to what happens in Hamburg, the things that happen here aren't worth worrying about. I think you guys just have a fantasy about the East and it makes you feel better about yourselves because it stops you from looking too hard about what the fuck is going on in your own homes. Really. You get off on it maybe. Maybe it's like a sex thing, which, you know, that's fine, but really it's not that bad. So. You had a bit of a holiday, you saw our sunset and the dawn rise in the white night and we caught the bad guys and everything is OK.

Everything is very good. Everything is very quiet. Everything is very calm.

Epilogue: London

Ignatius *and* **Caroline Stone***'s house. That night.*

Caroline There's no food. In the whole house. None. No bread. No beans. No fruit. No vegetables. No meat. Nothing.

Ignatius Fuck.

Caroline Yeah. I'm really sorry. I wasn't expecting you back.

Ignatius That's awful. I'm really hungry. What are we going to do?

Caroline Order a curry.

Ignatius Good idea.

Caroline Thank you.

Ignatius No, really. That's's a brilliant idea. I could kill a curry, actually. Yes.

Caroline Hey.

Ignatius What?

Caroline You.

Ignatius What?

Caroline Calm down.

Ignatius Sorry.

Caroline You're being a bit frenetic.

Ignatius I know. Sorry. I –

Caroline What?

Ignatius I missed you.

Caroline Yeah.

Ignatius Quite, can I say, rather a lot actually?

Caroline Me too.

Ignatius   I've only been gone a week. It seems longer than that.

Caroline   It does a bit, doesn't it?

Ignatius   It'll just take me a bit of time to readjust. I'm sorry. Am I being very strange?

Caroline   Just a little. It's OK. Take your time.

I went shopping with Mum last week.

Ignatius   Did you?

Caroline   She kept crying.

Ignatius   What?

Caroline   She came back for supper. She'd be talking perfectly normally about things and then she'd just start crying.

Ignatius   What was she crying about?

Caroline   She wouldn't say.

Ignatius   Oh.

Caroline   I know.

Ignatius   That sounds horrible. And a bit weird.

Caroline   Yeah. It was a bit.

So. Detective Stone.

Ignatius   So.

Caroline   How's the world?

Ignatius   Fucking . . .

He trails off.

Caroline   How was Germany?

Ignatius   It was good. We were busy. I didn't see much of it.

Caroline   What was Tallinn like?

Ignatius   Yeah. You know?

What's happening to the windows?

Caroline   They're kind of falling in.

Ignatius   Fuck.

Caroline   I know.

Ignatius   We should get that sorted.

Caroline   Yeah.

Your face looks completely fucked.

Ignatius   It is a bit. It'll heal.

Caroline   Ouch.

Ignatius   I used to think.

Caroline   What?

Ignatius   I used to think we should go somewhere again, me and you. On like a big holiday or something.

Caroline   I know. You talk about that all the time.

Ignatius   I missed the point, didn't I?

Some time. They look at each other.

Sometimes –

Caroline   What?

Ignatius   Do you ever get that feeling?

Caroline   What feeling's that?

Ignatius   I can't find the –

I'm –

She rests her fingers on his lips to stop him from trying to speak. Smiles at him. Rests her head on him, perhaps.